Special Educational Needs and the Internet

Issues for the Inclusive Classroom

Edited by Chris Abbott

London and New York

First published 2002
by RoutledgeFalmer
11 New Fetter Lane, London EC4P 4EE

Simultaneously published in the USA and Canada
by RoutledgeFalmer
29 West 35th Street, New York, NY 10001

RoutledgeFalmer is an imprint of the Taylor & Francis Group

© 2002 Selection and editorial matter, Chris Abbott;
individual chapters, the contributors
Typeset in Bembo by
Keystroke, Jacaranda Lodge, Wolverhampton
Printed and bound in Great Britain by
TJ International Ltd, Padstow, Cornwall

British Library Cataloguing in Publication Data
A catalogue record for this book is available from the British Library

Library of Congress Cataloging in Publication Data
A catalog record for this book has been requested

ISBN 0–415–26801–X (hbk)
ISBN 0–415–26802–8 (pbk)

For Hazel

Contents

Illustrations

Contributors

Chris Abbott is a lecturer in ICT education in the Department of Education, King's College London. Prior to joining King's College he was the Director of the Inner London Educational Computing Centre. His book *ICT: Changing Education* was published by RoutledgeFalmer in 2000.

Ken Carter is Chief Executive of the Deafax Trust, which is based within the School of Education, University of Reading. He is also the Director of the Deafax ICT Research Programme and helped to create Deafchild UK and Deafchild International.

Mel Farrar was a head teacher for almost twenty-nine years, opening (and closing) Foxdenton School and Integrated Nursery, Oldham. He is now Director of Foxdenton Ventures which continues the school's training and consultancy work in relation to excellence and quality management.

David Fettes has taught in mainstream and special schools for seventeen years. He currently teaches children with severe learning difficulties and autism, co-ordinates ICT and AAC and is a teacher mentor. He has postgraduate diplomas in special educational needs (SEN) and SLD and is studying for one in autism. His interests include literacy, psychology and the Internet.

John Galloway is the advisory teacher for ICT and special educational needs in the London Borough of Tower Hamlets. He is a behaviour specialist who has also delivered training and written materials on ICT and literacy difficulties.

Carolyn Howitt is COMPASS Education Editor at the British Museum, London.

Matthew James, who is profoundly deaf, is the Director of Operations for the Deafax Trust and Programme Director of Deafchild International. With the support of Cable and Wireless, he has worked with deaf and hearing children worldwide in ICT education and training.

Helen Lansdown is Programmes Director of Deafchild UK, which is part of the Deafax Trust. She is an experienced educational interpreter, and she also co-ordinates and helps to deliver TTA/NOF ICT teacher training and other literacy and communication programmes.

Jodi Mattes was a member of the British Museum COMPASS development team and is now Talking Images Project Officer, at the Royal National Institute for the Blind.

Sally Paveley is an ICT/SEN consultant based at the Advisory Unit, Hatfield, and also teaches part-time at Rosemary School in the London Borough of Islington.

Anne Phelan is National Co-ordinator of Special Needs and Finance at the National Centre for Technology in Education (NCTE), Dublin, Ireland. Prior to joining the NCTE she managed educational research projects investigating distance learning applications of new technology in education.

Maggie Pollard has been head teacher of Richmond Park School since 1989. She has been a member of many national committees on education and was a governor of the Scottish Council for Education and Technology (SCET) for several years. She was awarded an OBE in 2000 for services to children with special educational needs.

Chris Stevens has taught in mainstream and special schools, as deputy head and head teacher. He was Professional Officer for Special Educational Needs at the School Curriculum and Assessment Authority (SCAA). At SCAA he was responsible for extending access both to the curriculum and to recognition of achievement. He has been Head of Special Educational Needs and Inclusion at NCET/BECTA since 1996.

Terry Waller is a member of the special educational needs and inclusion team at BECTA and has been closely involved in the development of the UK Inclusion Web site. He has worked for BECTA and its predecessor NCET for over ten years.

David Ware is ICT co-ordinator at Little Heath School in the London Borough of Redbridge. He has been a teacher for twenty-five years, working in mainstream and special needs settings and local authority advisory services. He is committed to the principle that if we can get it right for young people with special educational needs we can get it right for everyone.

Acknowledgements

Chapters 2 and 6 appeared in an earlier form as *Making the Web Special* (published by King's College London and the Institute of Education) and *Making Communication Special* (published by King's College London). These publications were supported by the Viscount Nuffield Auxiliary Fund. Thanks to the SEN and ICT advisory community, including Alan Giles, Pauline Gorman and Ivor Finch, with whom I first investigated this area. Thanks are also due to all my colleagues and students in special schools and mainstream SEN support, with thanks for their support and encouragement. Thanks also to the Specialpedagogiska Institutet, Stockholm, Sweden, for Pictogram symbols; Widgit Software for Writing with Symbols 2000 symbols; Widgit Software and SENJIT for screen images from the Rara Avis Rainforest Web site; Mandeville School, Ealing, for the screen image from the school Web site.

Acronyms

AAC	Alternative and Augmentative Communication
ADD/ADHL	Attention Deficit Disorder/Attention Deficit Hyperactivity Disorder
ALT text	Alternative Text
ADSL	Asymmetrical Digital Subscriber Line
ASHA	American Speech-Language-Hearing Association
Becta	British Educational Communications and Technology Agency
Betsie	BBC Education Text to Speech Internet Enhancer
BSL	British Sign Language
CAST	Centre for Applied Specialist Technology
COMPASS	Collections Multimedia Public Access System
CPD	Continuous Professional Development
DfEE	Department for Education and Employment
DfES	Department for Education and Skills
EAL	English as an Additional Language
EBD	Emotionally and Behaviourally Disturbed
EFQM	European Framework for Quality Management
GIF	Graphics Interchange Format
HTML	Hyper Text Mark-Up Language
IATSE	Irish Association of Teachers in Special Education
ICT	Information and Communication Technology
IEP	Individualised Educational Plan
INSET	In-service Training
IP	Internet Protocol
IRC	Internet Relay Chat
ISDN	Integrated Services Digital Network
ISP	Internet Service Provider
IT	Information Technology

LEA	Local Education Authority
NCCA	National Council for Curriculum and Assessment
NCET	National Council for Educational Technology
NCTE	National Centre for Technology in Education
NGfL	National Grid for Learning
NOF	New Opportunities Fund
NQT	Newly Qualified Teachers
OECD/CERI	Organisation for Economic Co-operation and Development's Centre for Educational Research and Innovation
OFSTED	Office for Standards in Education
PDF	Post-script Data File
PE	Physical Education
PMLD	Profound Multiple Learning Difficulties
PRU	Pupil Referral Unit
PSDN	Public Switched Data Network
QCA	Qualifications and Curriculum Authority
RE	Religious Education
RNIB	Royal National Institute for the Blind
SAMI	Synchronized Accessible Media Interchange
SEN	Special Educational Needs
SENCO	Special Educational Needs Co-Ordinators
SENIT	Special Educational Needs Information Technology
SIP	Schools Integration Project
SLD	Severe Learning Difficulties
SMIL	Synchronized Multimedia Integration Language
STEPS	Support Teaching and Education Psychology Service
TCL	Telecommunications and Literacy
TTA	Teacher Training Agency
URL	Uniform Resource Locator
WAACIS	Wigram Aid to Ability for Critically-disabled Internet Students
WAI	Web Accessibility Initiative
WWS	Writing With Symbols

Chapter 1

Making the Internet special

Chris Abbott

Those of us who have based our careers around the support and education of young people with special educational needs (SEN) have seen far-reaching changes in our understandings and hopes for the children we serve. Many of the writers who have contributed to this book are based in special schools which might once have been seen as separatist or non-integrated provision. It is evident from the experiences and understandings they share here that a special school now is quite different from those of ten or twenty years ago.

Inclusion is not about building ramps or changing laws, it is an outcome of a developing understanding about the entitlement of all young people to the same standard of education. That understanding developed quickly in many special schools, and it is perhaps paradoxical that many inclusive practices have in fact arisen from the activities of those institutions.

Many UK special schools were opened in the later years of the nineteenth century and were the product of the efforts of enlightened individuals who were working within the system in order to change it. Forgotten pioneers, like Miss Bennett, who opened a school in the bandstand in Battersea Park, London, for local children who were TB carriers and banned from school, had as their aim the eventual inclusion of the children they taught into mainstream education.

In the same way, teachers and carers in special schools today strive to ensure that the young people for whom they are responsible are able to be included as fully as possible in the educational and social life of the community that surrounds them. There is much to be achieved, of course, and too often separation is an end rather than a beginning. It is too often true that:

> we live in a culture in which children are removed from one school and placed in another just because their differences are deemed

unacceptable, although usually there will be a paucity of evidence to suggest that this will result in any kind of success.

(Billington 2000: 2)

Many of the contributors to this book might agree with this analysis but they cannot change the situation alone; what they are able to do, and are doing with a pragmatic zeal which is to be commended, is to include the excluded, and to go some way to provide opportunities where the state may be deemed to have taken these away.

In his discussion of what he terms the 'pathologising' of children, by which they are named and then categorised, Billington (2000) is critical in particular of the rise of the 'expert' within psychology and education. He asserts that too often experts base their knowledge on their position within the power structure rather than on science. They 'lay claim not merely to science, but to fact, truth and reason' (Billington 2000: 29). The experts he is thinking of are presumably those who are responsible for allocating students to institutions: educational psychologists, social workers, LEA officers and all the panoply of the municipal bureaucracy. Those are not the experts who have contributed to this book; the writers here are teachers and head teachers, or people who go into classrooms on a daily basis; their credibility is without question and their voices are too seldom heard.

This book is about inclusion and entitlement, not about technology. Technologies are more or less visible depending upon our familiarity with them. I took my pump-action fountain pen totally for granted when I was at school, but today I would need to show a young person how to fill it. Similarly, the courses I used to run for teachers explaining how to move a computer mouse or start a program are entirely redundant, since those skills have become commonplace and no longer need to be learned.

However, not everyone has the easy access to technology that many in the developed world take for granted. Although much effort has been put into making existing technologies inclusive and available, newer developments do not always consider this matter as carefully as they might. The Internet, a catch-all term for an ever-changing gathering of allied but different tools, technologies and practices, is the focus here; but much that is said arises from our past understandings of the mutually advantageous links between ICT and SEN (Hawkridge and Vincent 1992; Blamires 1999; McKeown 2000).

Previous writing on the benefits of the Internet in school (Grey 1999) has indicated something of the range of possibilities in this area for pupils with special educational needs. One publication (Banes and Walter 2000) has begun to discuss the Internet with the needs of a specific group of learners in mind, and it is no surprise that several of the writers here have mentioned that book and the work of its authors at Meldreth Manor School, a pioneer institution in the use of the Internet in special education.

This publication aims to take that work forward by sharing a range of strategies and practices that developed in the 1990s around the use of the Internet in SEN settings, and particularly where the aim is to promote and enhance inclusion.

Models of technology use within special education, and in order to support inclusion, have varied greatly over the 1980s and 1990s. We have largely moved on from any simplistic notion of the computer as a teaching machine, although some of the hype surrounding integrated learning systems bears strong similarities to that era of understanding. It was depressing if unsurprising to see in the early years of the Web, the mid-1990s, a small revival of discredited 'drill and skill' software, this time in the form of small applets on Web pages. Just as some of the early computer software seemed to exist in order to provide a showcase for its programmer, so did some of those short-lived on-line skills programs. The full story of those years has been told elsewhere (Abbott 2000) but it as well here to remember that so much in education is cyclical. With new technologies we always need to be on our guard lest we are offered once again the discredited and unhelpful practices of the past.

It is sometimes helpful to be reminded (Papert 1996) of the ways in which our understanding of the role of computers in education has developed. The 1970s and 1980s saw the beginnings of the use of computers to support learning, rather than the study of computers as an end in itself. That early experimental stage of what was often called computer-assisted learning was linked, too often, with a simplistic belief in the ability of machines to teach. As has been shown (Abbott 2000), it took many years for the tool metaphor to become accepted and it is still not universal. It is hardly surprising therefore that some educators have made the mistake of thinking the Internet can, by itself, teach students. It is simply the latest manifestation of an ICT tool, albeit one with considerably more potential than many of its forebears.

Such simplistic belief in the power of the machine would not be acceptable to any of the contributors to this book, all of whom place ICT at the centre of their teaching. Even more than this, their experience and understanding enable them to see how the Internet can promote inclusion, provide entitlement and build on achievement. They write from different perspectives, as teachers, managers, advisers or resource providers, but all have as the centre of their work the learner's needs and a fundamental belief in inclusion for all.

We begin with the Web, perhaps the Internet phenomenon which above all others has brought the on-line world to prominence over the last decade. Not even invented at the beginning of the 1990s, the Web is now an all-pervasive presence in much of the developed world, where no advertisement is unaccompanied by a Web address and no television programme fails to have an associated Web site. The focus of the first part of the book is the use of the Web to gather and, more especially, to publish information.

There are particular issues that arise from Web use and these form the focus of the next chapter. Building a school or centre Web site is a process requiring much planning and thought: not so much about the technical processes, for that expertise can be purchased, but in order to consider what information should be published and why the school may need a Web site in the first place. It is a natural impulse to seek to celebrate the achievements of students, but this can be an area where careful thought is needed, especially if names and photographs are to be published on the Web. The chapter goes on to offer guidance in this area, and to suggest ways of ensuring that the site finds its intended audience.

Chapter 3, written from the perspective of a special school ICT co-ordinator, takes the process further. David Fettes explains how one severe learning difficulties (SLD) school set up a Web site which was aimed to be not so much a publicity agent for the school as a tool for learning to be used by the students. He explains how different groups of staff were involved in the process and the kind of planning that was needed to ensure that this was successful. As a classroom teacher Fettes is only too aware of the problems and challenges that arise as learners with a wide range of needs begin to access the Web, and he offers a variety of strategies to help other schools facing the same difficulties.

The British Museum is a much larger institution than Mandeville School but also has the needs of SEN learners very much in mind. Many large museums have developed extensive education Web sites and several have attempted to ensure that the needs of all learners are met in some way, but the British Museum was determined to plan entitlement of this kind from the beginning.

In Chapter 4 Carolyn Howitt and her colleague Jodi Mattes, who is now based at the Royal National Institute for the Blind, describe the importance of considering the needs of all users from the earliest stages of a project. They explain how their first priority was to ensure that the on-line collections database was accessible to visually impaired and blind users. They provide clear advice about screen readers and parallel text-only pages, as well as explaining the use of other text enhancement tools. Their project then went on to consider the needs of students with learning difficulties and, working with a partner special school, a further version of the collections database was developed. Learners in mainstream schools who have special needs were not forgotten either, and Howitt and Mattes explain how they built differentiation into their museum resource centre.

Sally Paveley divides her time between teaching in a special school and training special needs teachers to use ICT, so she is well placed to consider strategies for improving access to the Web. In Chapter 5 she explains how she has built on earlier understanding about accessing ICT in order to develop a range of approaches to the Web for students with learning difficulties. School intranets are considered, as are switch access and the need for usage agreements.

Part II deals with communicating information, very often through the use of e-mail, but increasingly through other tools, technologies and practices such as video-conferencing, fax, Web telephony or recorded video. Chapter 6 looks at the area of communication in general and notes that the entitlement to communicate is a basic human right.

The Internet is not the first communicative technology to which schools have had access, and valuable lessons can be learnt from the use of fax and telephone. E-mail is entering a new era for many users as symbol e-mail becomes possible, and this is discussed alongside newer on-line communicative practices such as chat in some of its many forms.

Some schools have built on the use of e-mail to extend and develop the curriculum for their pupils and include them more fully in the wider world. In Chapter 7 David Ware writes about how this has been done at one school for children with learning difficulties, and he explains why the school feels that this area is so important. With particular emphasis on the school's very successful use of the Travel Buddies model, Ware provides guidelines and case studies to illustrate a wide range of different approaches to the curricular use of e-mail.

Ken Carter and his colleagues have been keen users of the fax machine through the innovative projects with which they have been involved while working with the deaf community. Many past technologies have been particularly exclusive of the deaf and hearing-impaired, but access to ICT and the Internet can be promoted for this group as the authors of Chapter 8 show. Carter, James and Lansdown describe the development of an on-line resource area for those who are deaf or have a hearing impairment. They also explain the work of the research unit they have set up to investigate the use of ICT in inclusive environments.

As the head teacher of a special school in Glasgow, Maggie Pollard is well placed to give an overview of the use of the Internet in her school, an institution well known as a centre of excellence in this area. With strong reliance on the power of a good story, and belief in the entitlement of her students to gain access to their local environment, Pollard explains how the story of five swans was able to do just that. The school puts a strong emphasis on the importance of the arts: beautiful displays fill the classrooms and corridors, and music and drama have a major role in the curriculum. ICT and the Internet are used in innovative ways during arts activities, always linked with the school's key principles, which are described in the chapter.

Part III deals with the vital policy and management issues which must be considered in this area. It begins with a discussion of the implications of the broadband connections which have recently arrived in schools. Such fast connection speeds have the potential to offer an Internet experience which is as much connected with video, audio and images as with text or even symbols.

Chapter 10 looks in more detail at the topic of symbols, the alternative systems of communication and literacy which have helped to include more and more students in education, recreation and daily life. Symbols provide access to communication and literacy, and as they begin to be more visible on the Internet it is important that all resource providers are encouraged to take note of the needs of this group.

The chapter also describes how the rapid improvement in connection speeds has led to changing practices in areas where it has been installed for some time, and then raises some of the important issues for schools seeking to use broadband Internet safely and successfully.

Mel Farrar ran a very successful special school in Oldham, north-west England, until it was amalgamated. He describes in Chapter 11 how the school's beliefs were reflected in the ways in which it has used ICT and the Internet to promote its activities and celebrate achievement. Recent years have seen a rapid increase in the number of curriculum and consumer awards that can be won by institutions such as schools, and Foxdenton was very successful in this area. Farrar explains how the school Web site was crucial to this success and enabled the school to present itself as it wished rather than through the eyes and words of others.

Becta is the UK agency charged by the government with responsibility for supporting all aspects of ICT in the education system. Becta, and its predecessor NCET, have both been lucky enough to have access to members of staff with particular knowledge of the SEN and inclusion area. When Becta was asked to take over responsibility for the National Grid for Learning (NGfL) it was not long before plans were laid for the ambitious Inclusion site. In Chapter 12 Terry Waller, a long-time NCET and Becta stalwart, and Chris Stevens, now at Becta after being responsible for SEN in the curriculum at a government agency, describe the development of national resources to support teachers who are committed to inclusion. They explain the differing ways in which mailing lists and Web sites can provide support, and some of the thinking behind the Inclusion site. They also offer a valuable summary of the ways in which government has sought to legislate and intervene in this area, and the chapter illustrates the framework within which the work described in the other chapters has been able to take place.

John Galloway works as an SEN advisory teacher in a local education authority, but he too has a strategic role, although across a smaller range of schools and with a need to provide locally tailored rather than national resources. In Chapter 13 he focuses on Web support for inclusion at local or LEA level, using examples not just from his own area but from other developments around the UK. LEA intranets are another focus of this chapter as Galloway discusses what should be provided nationally and what is better developed as a locally based resource.

The last contributed chapter is, quite rightly, from outside the UK, since it deals with the wider and international view on inclusion. Anne Phelan has responsibility for special needs at the National Council for Technology in Education (NCTE), the Irish government's equivalent of Becta. In Chapter 14 Phelan places SEN activity on the Web within the wider international context, as well as discussing the innovative experiences of Irish educators.

The book ends with a chapter looking to the future and indicating the wider changes in schooling set in train by the use of the Internet in education – and the literacy practices that are likely to form a response to these developments.

When they wrote their far-sighted book on learning difficulties and computers, Hawkridge and Vincent (1992) concluded with a discussion of networking. Their intention was to discuss human networking, the linking together of expertise and experience which is so vital and yet so difficult to establish. Their words, however, could also apply to the Internet, the on-line network which was to become established soon after their book was published.

Networking must be made effective. It can bring essential resources into the classroom. Teachers will be helped to exploit computers for children and adults with learning difficulties. These learners will have better access to the curriculum. To policy-makers, the issues appear not nearly as urgent as they seem to the teachers and learners. The stones in the river do not know how hot it is out on the hill.

(Hawkridge and Vincent 1992: 223)

Policy makers, not only in the UK but in much of the developed world, have seen the Internet as an urgent issue. The international race to be the most connected country, or the one with the fewest students for each computer, or the one where the most people in education belong to on-line message boards, has been in progress for some years now, with little sign of any finishing post on the horizon. Similarly, but with rather less urgency, governments have indicated their commitment to the inclusive ideal, but many observers have seen a slowing of progress in this area. In the UK, particularly, competing initiatives regarding league tables, 'standards' and school inspections have left inclusion as the forgotten policy (Abbott 2001). It is hoped that the work of the contributors to this book, and their colleagues, will help to speed us on the way to ever more inclusive practices in education.

References

Abbott, C. (2000) *ICT: Changing Education*, London: RoutledgeFalmer.

Abbott, C. (2001) 'Special educational needs: becoming more inclusive' in J. Dillon and M. Maguire (eds) *Becoming a Teacher: Issues in Secondary Teaching*, second edition, Buckingham: Open University Press.

Banes, D., and Walter, R. (2000) *Internet for All*, London: David Fulton.

Billington, T. (2000) *Separating, Losing and Excluding Children: Narratives of Difference*, London: RoutledgeFalmer.

Blamires, M. (ed.) (1999) *Enabling Technology for Inclusion*, London: Paul Chapman.

Grey, D. (1999) *The Internet in School*, London: Cassell.

Hawkridge, D., and Vincent, T. (1992) *Learning Difficulties and Computers: Access to the Curriculum*, London: Jessica Kingsley.

McKeown, S. (2000) *Unlocking Potential: How ICT can Support Children with Special Educational Needs*, Birmingham: Questions Publishing.

Papert, S. (1996) *The Connected Family: Bridging the Generation Gap*, Atlanta GA: Longstreet Press.

Part I

Gathering and publishing information

Chapter 2

Making the Web special

Chris Abbott

The World Wide Web offers unparalleled opportunities for special schools to share resources and inform parents, other agencies and the wider community. Although Web practice is still developing, some important guidelines have already been established, and these are discussed here.

Since its invention in the early 1990s the World Wide Web has rapidly expanded, and we have now reached the stage where no advertisement, feature film or television programme seems complete without its associated Web site. Radio hosts invite their listeners to visit the Web and join in discussions, advertising hoardings promise extra information or the chance to win prizes if Web sites are visited, and airlines sell tickets cheaper through the Web than through any other medium. Web-based sales, in particular, developed quickly at the end of the 1990s and have become, despite some misgivings, an established part of purchasing practice in countries such as the UK.

Many schools have also begun to investigate the potential of the Web, although more have used it to try to find information than have done so as a publishing medium. This is unfortunate, as it offers considerable possibilities for sharing information, publicising achievement and celebrating success. Schools that began to explore Web publication in the 1990s have, in many cases, developed a range of innovative practices that can inspire others who may be considering this area. Many of those pioneer schools are mentioned in this book.

Special schools or pupil referral units may be considering the on-line publication of a range of different information and resources. There is no need to be concerned that the process of getting information on to the Web sounds complicated: the really important questions for those in schools to answer relate to what should go on the site, not the technicalities of getting it there. In any case, a ready source of assistance in this area will probably be found in the form of local mainstream school students or even the children of staff members. With the development of Web editing programs, many special educational needs (SEN) students will also be able to create their own pages or make resources for the school site.

What do you want to share or publish?

For many schools, the starting point for developing a Web site is to put the school brochure on-line. There are many ways to do this. Most schools and units choose to rearrange the contents of the brochure, perhaps providing internal links so that it is easy to go from one place to another and jump back to the beginning. Others redesign their brochure for its appearance on-line, and take the opportunity to include information which can be changed frequently and which would be impossible to include in the printed version. There are many special school and pupil referral unit (PRU) Web sites listed on the King's College Internet and Special Schools site (www.sed.kcl.ac.uk/special), and some time spent browsing through these will provide some useful ideas for schools who may be at an earlier stage.

Calthorpe School in Birmingham is an example of a school which has published a wide range of information about its facilities on the Web (www.calthorpe.bham.sch.uk). Some schools are generous enough to include their curriculum policies or other useful information on their Web site. A good example of this kind of site is the Royal Blind School, Edinburgh (www.royalblindschool.org.uk), where a guide to assistive technologies is included alongside a profile of the school.

Having your brochure on-line can be very helpful; parents who have access to the Internet can read all about prospective schools before visiting, other schools can compare how their colleagues approach matters, and the school can raise its own profile. It is important that steps are taken to ensure that the site will be kept up to date and that information which is no longer relevant will be removed; a site containing outdated information presents a worse image of a school than does the absence of a Web site.

Celebrating the achievements of your students

A next step for many schools is to put on-line a selection of work by pupils: this may be writing, artwork or even sound or video files. This can be an exciting way to reach out to the wider community and allow others to see what you and your students have achieved. The newsletter on the Springwell Dene School Web site (homepages.enterprise.net/springwelldene), for example, usually includes photographs and examples of recent work by students.

If you do display work, it is important to change it regularly and to make sure that it is shown to its best advantage. Displaying writing is relatively straightforward and you can be sure that it will be accessible to others, as it is the end user of a Web browser who decides on the size and style of font to be used. This is an important point, and many schools have not discovered that it is not necessary to read Web pages in ten-point Roman typeface just because that is the default setting on the software. Changing to a bigger and simpler font can help many readers. As the designer of a page, you can choose to display headings and titles in different sizes, and these relative sizes will remain in use whatever font choices are made by your readers.

You will also need to grapple with the difficult question of whether or not to attach the name of the student whose work is being displayed. In most cases, it would seem logical to do so, but be aware that you are publishing this information internationally – and locally. Would you be happy for the same information to appear with the pupil's name in your local newspaper – and in an international magazine? If so, then it is probably acceptable to use the name on the Web site.

Whether or not you will seek parental permission will depend on custom and practice at the school and on the age of the student. However, be particularly careful about publishing attributed writing which may include personal details about home life. Do you really want to give a full physical description of a student together with a list of interests to anyone who may read the site? Many schools take the careful approach and use only first names, and do not identify younger pupils in photographs. You may feel this is too cautious, but it is a decision which should be taken at senior management level and not left to the ICT co-ordinator.

Resources and expertise of the school

You will certainly wish to celebrate the achievements of your school, and may even decide to link to other on-line information which relates to you. Many schools still do not realise that OFSTED reports and DfES performance and truancy tables are all available on-line, and if you are pleased with how these represent you, you may want to consider linking to them. Some schools link to the OFSTED site so that the whole report is available, but others choose to offer a few well chosen phrases together with their comments on the inspection; a chance, perhaps to add that commentary which cannot be attached to the original report.

Some schools use their Web site to share resources with others, to make available the expertise available in the school, and even to advertise services such as INSET and publications. An example of a well developed site such as this is Kingsbury School in Lancashire (www.sldonline.org/Kingsbury), where a wide range of resources is made available within a symbol-based environment. An extensive range of planning and policy documents can all be downloaded.

Knockevin School in Northern Ireland has been developing the use of presentation software to make talking books, and this is described on its Web site (www.knockevin.com). Not all information is appropriate to those outside the school community, and Chailey Heritage School (www.pavilion.co.uk/chailey) is an example of a site where information about homework and school plans is available, but only to those who are registered to the site. In this way, students and their parents can have access to information which is both relevant and private to them as a group – the present-day equivalent to taking a letter home, but with rather less potential for getting lost on the way.

Many on-line resources are lengthy documents and for that reason they are available in Adobe Acrobat format. This is the format in which OFSTED puts school reports on the Web, so you may have come across it already. To read a document in this format (you will recognise it as the file name will end with .pdf) you need the Adobe Acrobat reader software – but the good news is that it is free. Most sites which use Acrobat files also include a button to link to the site where you can download the reader software, and it is well worth doing so, if only so that you can read all those OFSTED reports on your neighbouring schools, or the one where you are thinking of applying for a job!

Daniel House Pupil Referral Unit (www.carberry.demon.co.uk) offers a wide range of resources, including lesson plans and other information for teaching students about the Internet and Web site design.

Sound and movement are beginning to become more common too: the sensory garden site from Blackfriars School (www.sln.org.uk/ blackfriars) includes the sound of birdsong as well as flowers that grow before your eyes.

Some schools offer to make available their Word, Clicker and Powerpoint program files to other schools, an excellent example of the way in which special schools can support each other. It is this use of the Web which is likely to interest schools moving towards the model of specialist schools as resource centres for the wider educational community, a model which is encouraged by UK government policy.

Why use the World Wide Web?

Finding a way of sharing resources is often one of the most difficult parts of the process of becoming a specialist centre for others, and creating a Web site is a cost-effective, developmental and wide-ranging solution to that problem.

One of the most compelling reasons for putting information on the Web is that it can be constantly changed with little effort and almost no cost. Keeping a printed brochure up to date is an expensive process, involving annual reprints or cumbersome systems of yearly inserts. A Web site, by comparison, exists only as a set of computer files, and we all know how easily they can be updated and amended. They can also be lost, of course, so please don't forget the backups – and the backups of those backups – which you keep in a different place or on a different computer.

Spotting a spelling error in a printed brochure is a heartsinking moment, accompanied by the realisation that it will be there to haunt you for the next year or two; a mistake on a Web site can be corrected in minutes and never seen again. Similarly, if the head teacher changes half-way through the year – or even, heaven forbid, changes his or her mind about something – the amendments can be added to the site immediately.

This ability to update is only part of the story, however; perhaps the main reason to have a Web site is to communicate with others – particularly parents and the local community. As many as 60 per cent of families in many schools have computers now, and almost as many have Internet access. You can even load an off-line version of your Web site on to computers in local libraries or other places which may have computers but do not yet have Internet access – the browser software to view the site is free, so no expense is involved.

Keeping in touch with parents can be a one-way process, with the school publishing information and parents reading it. It could be much more than that, however, and mainstream schools are beginning to experiment with putting feedback mechanisms on-line so that parents can contact the school, perhaps to check what homework has been set. If one of your local mainstream schools is doing this, why not link with them and add a copy of the form to your own site?

Special schools can also keep in touch, using the Web, with mainstream schools with which they may be linked, or which some of their pupils may have attended. Pupil referral units (PRUs) which have pupils on roll at a local secondary school can maintain links like this, and pupils can be helped to feel part of both institutions. Easy links between the sites involved in this way will help, and these could be in the form of Web rings or Net circles, as described below.

Structuring your site

There are no real fixed rules about Web sites – but there are some developing conventions which you may as well follow unless you are sure you have a better idea. Most sites, for example, have a page called index.html as a starting point. This is not just a matter of conformity as Web browsers will expect to find this file, although you do not need to quote it in your address. Not having to type index.html may not seem much, but losing ten key presses from what might be a very long address can be extremely helpful to some special needs and assistive technology users who may be using switch and scanning software. Mel Farrar gives an example of a well developed school Web site structure in Chapter 11.

Some schools have been very inventive about the way in which they design their pages. Longwill School (atschool.eduweb.co.uk/bday) has used the convention of a card index, but also added a welcome on the first page using British Sign Language, making this a bilingual Web site which is accessible to the deaf students at the school.

One difficult decision will relate to the extent to which you will use some of the technical possibilities such as frames, Java or other plug-ins. Frames are a convention whereby your screen splits into several areas – or frames – some of which stay on screen as an index or title bar while others show changing content. This all sounds fine and it can be a helpful way of involving your reader, but there are difficulties too. Not all browsers can cope with frames, although this is less of a problem now. More seriously, some users with special needs may not be able to navigate through a site with frames, and you may be making your site inaccessible to them. If you want to check the accessibility of your site, you can do so by sending it to Bobby (www.cast.org/bobby), and if it is accessible you will be sent back a logo which you can proudly display.

Some complex Web sites make use of applets or small programs which are usually written in the Java programming language. These will work only on later versions of the browser software, and where the user has enabled Java to be used. Some users prefer not to do this, as it can be very slow to load a Java Web site. It used to be considered polite – in Netiquette terms – at least to warn people through an introductory page that they are about to enter a Java-enhanced site, and to offer them the opportunity to choose instead a non-Java version; fewer sites offer this facility now.

Other enhanced facilities on sites may require the user to download other small programs, known as plug-ins, and this is fine if the user does not mind doing so – the basic versions of the programs are usually free and most sites add a link to the source of the program. These plug-ins may enable panoramic views of the school site, or audio and video inserts.

Who will be your audience?

One of the most important questions to ask is: who will be the primary audience for your Web site? It is almost impossible to produce a site which is equally suited to parents, pupils and other schools – let alone local education authorities (LEAs), OFSTED, local businesses and all the other interested parties who might want to know what you are doing.

One solution to this dilemma is to ask the different audiences to select their path when they connect to the site. Meldreth Manor (www.meldrethmanor.com), a school for pupils with severe learning difficulties, has taken this a stage further not only by making the site split into different sections for different audiences, but by making the pupil section accessible by the use of symbols for selection and by structuring the page so that switch users are not presented with difficulties.

Virtual communities

Much has been written about the potential of the Web and the Internet in general to allow people to reach out and link with others and communicate across what were previously unbridgeable boundaries. Although some of this is rightly criticised as overstated and exaggerated, it is still true that there are tremendous possibilities in this area. Even where the contacts that have been made antedate the Web, they can be enhanced by its use.

The notion of virtual communities, popularised by Rheingold (1993, 1996) and others (Jones 1995, 1997; Shields 1996), is one that has taken root and been recognised across a wide range of on-line practice. The 'cyberspace settlers' have indeed 'come *en masse*' as was predicted a few years ago (Rheingold 1996: 415). Virtual community is not a wholly positive development; drug dealers, anarchists and paedophiles can form virtual communities too. Despite this negative aspect of the phenomenon, the development of virtual community is one of those aspects of the Internet which bears least relation to previous practices. It would have been possible before the Internet for two special school teachers such as David Ware in Essex and Barbara Garrison in California to have linked up and begun exchanging work between their schools – but it would have been an extremely unlikely and unique occurrence. Since the Internet became available to schools, David's description in Chapter 7 of his school's links with California is but one example of an activity open to all schools, however small and isolated.

It has been shown (Abbott and Cribb 2001) that many professionals working within special education have previously felt isolated or out of touch with their mainstream colleagues, and this may be part of the reason for the sector's rapid acceptance of the on-line world; SEN teachers are entitled to inclusion as much as are the students they teach.

Most people find information on the Web – or fail to do so – by using search engines, indexing tools which try, and mostly fail, to keep up with the enormous amount of information added to the Web every day. They do this by the use of automated Bots, computer programs which spend all their time roaming around the world collecting information. You do not have to wait for a Bot to find you, however, as you can send information about your site to a search engine and specify the key words which may send users to your site. Sadly, this may not now be possible with some of the major search engines, since they have begun to charge high fees to resource providers who wish to be included. General search engines, in any case, are so wide-reaching now that it may be much more appropriate to ensure that the school site is listed on educational and SEN centres rather than through the global searching tools.

If you hope to get international interest you may have to be a little more inclusive in the language you use; elementary as well as primary, and K-12 (Kindergarten to Grade 12) as well as Key Stages 1 to 4. You may also have to include terms to describe special needs which we might feel are no longer acceptable here but may still be in common use elsewhere, such as retarded or remedial. These terms will not be visible on your site, but they will be present in the underlying code and the search engines will then find them. There are some sites which attempt to help you submit your site to many search engines at once; try searching on words like SUBMIT and SEARCH and you will find them, but no address is included here as these tend to change frequently.

There are some interesting ways for Web site owners to align themselves with others who are dealing with similar issues or concerns. Most of the major on-line portals like Yahoo and Excite offer clubs, Web rings or other ways of grouping sites together. In this way, if you find one site which interests you, you may find a string of others which also meet your needs. There are rings for all the major disabilities and many lesser-known ones, as well as specific educational groupings on educational sites.

You should also try to get yourself listed in as many places as possible. There are a number of listings of UK schools, for example, one of the largest being on the RM Learning Alive site (www.learningalive.co.uk). Any school can be listed there, as you do not have to be a subscriber to that Internet service. If you are a subscriber, you will be able to use unlimited Web space to create your site. Most LEAs also have sites now, and you will want to make sure that you are listed there.

There will probably be a local government or commercial site for your town or district too, and most will be keen to list you as a local organisation with a Web site. If you do not know what Web sites exist for your locality, type the name of your town into the Yahoo Web site (www.yahoo.co.uk) and see what comes up – but click on UK sites only or you will be offered all the other places around the world with the same name.

What next?

As more facilities appear on the Web, and particularly as faster connections become available in schools, exciting possibilities will open up for special schools and pupil referral units. Sites which at present consist of static text or images are being transformed into multimedia centres, with video and sound clips, complete recordings of school performances or even a video of a student achieving that hurdle which she has been working towards in Physical Education (PE) or Life Skills. Of course, you may not want to go as far as Frewen College (www.frewcoll.demon.co.uk), which uses its

Web pages, among other things, to advertise the use of the school buildings for conferences and wedding receptions.

As would be expected, there is considerable support for inclusion available on the many sites developed by the main UK agencies as well as from individual schools. The main emphasis of this chapter has been on the enterprising work of individual institutions, but the major source in this area is the Inclusion Site (inclusion.ngfl.gov.uk) and the story of the development of this site is told in Chapter 12 by Stevens and Waller.

Summary

- The World Wide Web is a truly democratic publishing medium which does not discriminate against small schools or those margin- alised by society.
- The Web has the potential to change lives and link the isolated and marginalised.
- It is the role of all of us in the special education sector, supported by enlightened bodies such as the Viscount Nuffield Auxiliary Fund, which supported the original Internet and special schools projects, to ensure that students make the best possible use of this exciting new opportunity.

References

Abbott, C., and Cribb, A. (2001) 'Special Schools, inclusion and the World Wide Web: the emerging research agenda', *British Journal of Educational Technology* 32 (3), 331–42.

Jones, S. G. (ed.) (1995) *Cybersociety: Computer-mediated Communication and Community*, London: Sage.

Jones, S. G. (ed.) (1997) *Virtual Culture: Identity and Communication in Cybersociety*, London: Sage.

Rheingold, H. (1993) *Virtual Communities: Homesteading on the Electronic Frontier*, New York: Harper Perennial.

Rheingold, H. (1996) 'A slice of my life in my virtual community' in P. Ludlow (ed.) *High Noon on the Electronic Frontier*, Cambridge MA: MIT Press.

Shields, R. (ed.) (1996) *Cultures of Internet: Virtual Spaces, Real Histories, Living Bodies*, London: Sage.

Chapter 3

Developing the school Web site as a tool for learning

David Fettes

David Fettes reflects on his experiences of developing a school Web site which aims to be inclusive of the needs of a wide range of children. He indicates the key principles to be borne in mind, as well as suggesting practical strategies for involving other staff and developing a school's inclusive on-line practice.

This chapter will explore the use of the school Web site (www.mandeville.ealing.sch.uk) for enhancing teaching and learning in Mandeville School in west London, a school for children with severe learning difficulties (SLD). I am the ICT co-ordinator as well as being a class teacher at the school. We decided that the primary audience for the main site would be our children and that the Web site would reflect their experience but would also be a window on the world (www.mandeville.ealing.sch.uk/page2.htm).

Constructing the site and involving staff

We decided to construct the site with simple page sequences reflecting the idea of a picture book, with no scrolling down required. Individual staff members preparing Web pages do not need to learn HTML, and more recently have been using Microsoft Word as an authoring tool. Involvement in authoring the pages tends to develop in a spiral fashion, sometimes driven by enthusiasts, at other times prompted by ICT training.

Phase 1   The enthusiasts

Initially teacher enthusiasts started making Web pages about their class and curriculum subjects. One spent a whole school holiday making a Web tour of Mandeville School (www.mandeville.ealing.sch.uk/leigh.html); more teachers then voluntarily made further sections. These staff could be considered enthusiasts, and my philosophy would be to get the enthusiasts involved first. As time has gone by some staff have left and new staff have arrived, and the enthusiast stage has been revisited several times, but on-going development of the Web site cannot rely solely on the enthusiasts.

Phase 2   Whole school training

I showed classroom support staff how to use our Web site; their response was that it would be more useful if the site included photographs of children in a wider range of classes, as children had better understanding and motivation when seeing photographs of themselves and their friends. I arranged for the teachers to produce a literacy section for the Web site with the help of an LEA adviser (www.mandeville.ealing.sch.uk/reading6.htm). I have so far targeted the Web page making mainly at the teachers because I feel that teachers should be able to make Web pages. The Teacher Training Agency standards (TTA 1998) emphasise the teacher making presentations for children. As there is not enough time in the normal school day for these types of activities, we rely heavily on staff volunteering to make them in their own time after school or at home, or in the limited non-contact time they have.

This training phase has been revisited during our New Opportunities Fund (NOF) ICT training. Our training, using the provider MpowerNet with myself as co-trainer, is being delivered using face-to-face training, and emphasises that the skills of using the Internet are basic skills for all teachers. All the teachers have completed a needs analysis exercise and the SLD-specific training has been localised to the school needs and differentiated to two levels for the more and the less confident staff. The NOF training and the increasing use of the Internet at home by staff have helped in increasing confidence, and part of the training involves making pages for the school site. The NOF training showed the need for further individual support for all teachers. Part of this takes the form of after-school sessions for teachers to prepare pages for the subjects they co-ordinate. These skills learned in training need to be generalised to the normal everyday classroom experience of teachers.

Phase 3 In-class support

I initially offered support to less confident teachers who none the less were interested in ICT. Children were encouraged to access our Web site using the mouse or touch screen and to see any photographs of themselves or classmates, and I then encouraged their teacher to base our sessions on developing Web pages related to current and successful topic work. Each week the children would bring something they had done on a topic like art and craft, and would be photographed with their work (www.mandeville.ealing.sch.uk/joseph4.htm).The children have then often quickly recognised themselves on the Web site.We are working on developing the children's skills in ICT and, as they develop their own recording using Writing with Symbols software and the digital camera, this will be incorporated into the Web site.

Planning and preparation

After experimenting with topic-based and class-based designs for the Web site we have settled for a subject-based design. Although this top level of subjects provides cognitive access mainly for the staff, the on-going activities and projects that children most easily engage with can easily be inserted under particular subjects. Concentrating on developing one aspect of the site at a time has been useful: the science section was recently developed and now includes sections on National Science Week, museums and natural history excursions (www.mandeville.ealing.sch.uk/science_home.htm). It would be useful to add a search facility. Simple drop-down menus have been added to the subject pages but these require the reading of small text, and experience has shown that children prefer locating pages using a grid of choices, ideally supported by pictures or symbols; our music section gives an example of this.

A related aspect is that of whole-school activities such as work on festivals or theme weeks.These provide a good focus for Web site development. I develop a section for these in advance of the event, incorporating aspects of the programme of activities, and this acts as an advance organiser for children and staff. Photographs taken during the event are put on the Web site the same day. As new sections are added to the Web site, posters are placed beside the computers and on the staff notice board, and the uniform resource locator (URL) is e-mailed to teachers to keep them up to date. On occasions the start page for the school Web browser is set to the current focus, or the intranet page is put in the computer's Startup folder, so that it is the first thing seen after the computer is switched on. Nothing beats actually showing staff new sections informally in order to develop enthusiasm, and staff also e-mail each other URLs that can inform the site development. It is important to discuss and plan the Web site so that it becomes more integrated into the way staff work. The Web editor may leave and the Web site would then stagnate if it had been kept going only through the efforts of one person.

Classroom management and the learning environment

The norm in many special school classrooms is one computer. With children with SLD we often have an adult based with the computer to facilitate use by between one and three children, while other children will work on other activities. In some classes this is difficult if the computer is such a strong motivator that children are distracted from their other work. Strategies to deal with this include using headphones, screening the computer or timetabling it so that such children are either using the computer or out of the room engaged on other activities. However, having the computer always in the room has made it less of a novelty and more of an everyday tool for many children.

Considerations for the teacher integrating the computer can be taxing. Have you organised the booking of the computer, logged in, checked the Web connection, and got the Web site up and running before the children arrive for the session? Do you know the Web site layout well? Can you help the children to navigate? Can you relate each picture to the children's experience? When the Internet connection fails, what does the teacher do? Switching to a school intranet which can contain all the content of the Internet Web site is one option: another approach is to use more than one computer.

Many National Grid for Learning (NGfL) funding schemes have paid for a single room to be wired for a small network, and this computer room may then be booked by classes. The advantage is that the computers are in place and only need switching on so that the whole class can access the same program – or the school Web site – or a differentiated range of activities can take place. In this way, it is simpler for the ICT co-ordinator to ensure all classes are getting access. The disadvantages are that most schools, including ours, are short of a room for the purpose. If this is the only model, there is a danger of ICT becoming separated from daily activities in classrooms. Our short-term goal is an Internet-connected computer in each classroom, backed up by providing extra access through timetabled free-standing computers. Our classrooms are wired with two or more network connection points, and this can enable more children to access the Web site simultaneously.

The introduction of literacy and numeracy frameworks, and the TTA ICT standards for teachers (TTA 1998), emphasise initial direct and interactive teaching in the first phase of each lesson. The provision of a large-screen monitor, or data projector system and interactive whiteboard, provides a useful way to explore the school Web site with a larger group or the whole class.

Web site-based tasks and approaches

I find a good way of integrating Web site-based activities is to set up a section of the site for a current or planned whole-school theme or activity. An example of this was our theme week on Switzerland. All the week's activities were based on the theme. In previous years the ICT activities were on stand-alone computers and could not be fully integrated with other aspects of the theme week; with the Internet this is now possible. A section of the Web site was set up with links to sites on the Heidi story, which we would be enacting, to sites showing pictures and videos of Switzerland and to a section to add pictures of the week as it unfolded. The Web site not only reflected the children's experience but became a mechanism for extending their world. The week was a success and the ICT component was able to complement it. Pictures of the children in the café, cooking Swiss food, and singing Swiss songs with a visitor from Switzerland were added on the day they were taken and the children were able to look at them on the Web site back in the classroom (www.mandeville.ealing.sch.uk/themeweek.htm).

This recording lent coherence to the on-going activities. It collected the different activities together and reinforced the point that they were linked through the topic of Switzerland. This is important for children with learning difficulties, as they do not necessarily realise that activities have an underlying link or purpose. Staff in each class were able to take the photographs, although it would be good to have a designated person touring the school to do this. Our children can see depicted the exact activities that they themselves have done but with other children doing them. The photographs also show that some children can remember activities for a year or more. Through this process we are able to build for our pupils a sense of community and an understanding that the other children are their schoolmates. Shared activities with other classes, such as Drama, reinforced a sense of community. Looking back on the activities on the Web site helps the children not only to remember the content of the activity but also to identify themselves, their classmates, the children and staff in other classes. A further development for this type of project, especially for our older children, would be to provide links to external sites with corresponding worksheets such as the activities described by De Cicco *et al.* (1999). The sheets could be made accessible to our children using screen shots and Makaton symbols. We are now developing a worksheet download section to the site (www.mandeville.ealing.sch.uk/brochure.htm).

The advantages of theme weeks must be weighed against their disadvantages. The theme week by definition lasts only a week and so work by staff on all activities could be thought to have a short lifetime. The next year's theme week will have a different focus. Is it worth it? I think it is, and it serves as a useful counterbalance at those times when the curriculum seems to be becoming more fragmented. The same approach has been taken in subsequent theme weeks on Religious Education (RE) and Drama (www.mandeville.ealing.sch.uk/re-week_home.htm and www.mandeville.ealing.sch.uk/themeweek2001-1.htm). Another useful aspect of school life to focus on is Religious Education. The school celebrates the main festivals of the major world religions, and the advantage of this for the Web site editor is that the same festivals will be celebrated the next year, so any external links we spend time finding should (if they still work) prove useful the following year (www.mandeville.ealing.sch.uk/re26.htm). I am now using this idea of reusability in many sections such as the farm visit (www.mandeville. ealing.sch.uk/animals-farm1.htm). The first hyperlink is to pictures of

Figure 3.1 The opening page of the farm site

the animals, and subsequent links are to particular visits. The first link will be useful with different classes over a long period of time.

When searching for external Web links to resources there is often a large difference in the suitability of material that can be found. For example, there is little on harvest festivals in the UK, although there is more on US sites, but a multitude of Christmas sites were found. Where external content is short I can put up suitable content on the school Web site, but this does require extra work in locating material and scanning. What would be really useful is a central database of links to age-sorted material on the Web for each subject area. Another useful resource link to put on the Web site RE section is one that enables printing out of pictures to colour away from the computer. Currently these are mainly links to external sites but we plan to make use of some of our artistic staff to make our own.

Christmas also proved to be a more fertile focus for links to more active Web pages with song sheets with MIDI musical accompaniment, and interactive Web pages with Java applet games. The children enjoyed these, and on some occasions the computer seemed to change character to be more like a television or tape recorder as children danced or sang along to the songs. The use of sound on Web pages has proved particularly motivating to our pupils with autism, and the majority of new pages are linked to a background MIDI file. The effect is often to increase the click-through time, where the child waits before clicking to the next page and so has more chance to absorb each page. Sound can also be a focus in itself, as can be seen in our music section on www.mandeville.ealing.sch.uk/page2.htm with links to well known songs and rhymes.

The longer-term aim would be to increase the access to interactive content so that the children had to do something to make the computer respond. Some exploratory pages have been made using JavaScript. In one activity the child has to type in its name, and the response is the appearance of a well known poem featuring the child's name and animated weather symbols (www.mandeville.ealing.sch.uk/hellojse.htm). In another, children have to enter six words about themselves next to the correct symbol and then click a button so that a screen appears showing a twenty-eight-word description incorporating the entered data, which can then be printed out as an 'About Me' piece. Other methods of input using symbols rather than text are being investigated. The level of task needed varies from cause and effect, where one would like the child to operate a switch or touch screen to cause an interesting and educational response from the computer, to animation and sound or speech. Other activities involve the child in selecting pictures, symbols or word buttons to enable choice and problem solving.

External links include, where possible, links to the Web sites of local places of worship that have been visited, and links to sites offering electronic cards for each festival. These can be sent between classes: the fact that they are often animated and musical and that the children can choose one from the selection of thumbnail pictures on the page seems to make them particularly satisfying to some children. This process also links communication with access to information and is a further aspect of ICT in which there is much investigation of the benefits to children with SLD, for example using symbols to fax or e-mail (Abbott, 1999).

I have made a separate section on the Web site for external links for the children to use (www.mandeville.ealing.sch.uk/linkspage-kids.htm). It uses a symbol grid arranged around subjects. This has not been as useful as hoped because of several factors, including the difficulty of finding child-friendly sites to link to and the lack of contextualisation of those links. It will perhaps be better to put the links on each of our subject sections. Another opportunity for integrating the Web site into class work arises when a visitor comes into school over a period. A dental hygienist came in for one session a week for a month, and the Web site recorded the sessions as they proceeded. Having the expert in to run the sessions also freed the class teachers more than usual to take photographs of the session. The Web site section incorporated Makaton symbols to increase understanding and access to the health messages (www.mandeville.ealing.sch.uk/pse-food9.htm).

Looking at the school Web site does not only hold benefits for the children: the staff can see what other classes are doing, where they have been on outings and if they look suitable for their own classes. The current plan is to involve children increasingly in the design and production of Web pages. It is true to say that we are only at the beginning of this and other schools will be far in advance of us. Some children are able to use the digital camera and especially enjoy seeing the photograph uploaded to the computer. The clarity is surprising to the children and they enjoy noticing things on the uploaded image that they had not on the item photographed, such as a tiny picture on a child's dress.

Differentiation and accessibility (cognitive, physical and sensory)

Our classes have a wide spread of attainment and need, and accessibility of the school Web site is an important area for us. While learning the basics of Web development we initially focused on access to the more advanced children in terms of cognitive development and those without severe physical or visual secondary disabilities. In the area of cognitive access many children can recognise the photographs on the Web site pages, a fair number can recognise the Makaton symbols used, and a minority can read the captions. A number of our pupils with autism are able to read, and an increasing number of others are starting to learn to do so. Some children are not yet able to recognise the photographs of themselves but are able to recognise themselves in a large simple familiar photograph or on a familiar video. On-going work on photograph recognition with these children should allow them in time to access the current style of page, although other styles such as smaller photographs linked to a large photograph will be tried. These children would also benefit from the presence of video clips, sound and animations.

It is planned to enable access by children at earlier cognitive levels by these approaches and by the on-screen photographs being shown concurrently with a corresponding real-life experience perhaps by viewing a cookery section each week during the actual cookery lesson. Collecting the objects associated with a Web site section in a pack to be used alongside the computer may also enable understanding (Banes and Walter 2000). For children at early stages of cognitive development, Web site sections (without names) about each child may be most relevant.

Another aspect of cognitive access is the navigation of the site. Children find it easier to navigate Web sites where navigation choices are laid out consistently. Hierarchical linking is easier to understand compared with those sites that employ cross-linking. However, the depth of hierarchical linking can prove a problem and has been investigated in symbol communication devices (Miller et al., 1999) with regard to looking for a particular piece of information. One solution is a contents page for longer linear sections, allowing the user to jump in at the correct place. We have found that some of our pupils with autism do systematically explore the Web site and, having found items of interest, at a later date are able to quickly navigate to their favourite sections.

Switch access is possible via a simple mouser box into which a switch as well as a mouse can be fixed, and also by writing keyboard access into the HTML. Some schools like Meldreth Manor (www.meldrethmanor. com) have extensive experience in this area. With children with additional severe visual difficulties, of which there are a small number in the school, it would be appropriate if Web pages could be read out through the use of screen-reading software. We are aware that our Web site does not fully meet recommendations for access by visually impaired people. We do have some pupils with hearing impairment, and they are able to access the current Web site with its use of photographs and symbols.

In other ICT programs they may be frustrated where the only response to their action or choice is a sound effect which they cannot hear, so this must be borne in mind when developing the Web site further. Such pupils do benefit from seeing signs on screen and this is possible using animated GIFs (www.britishsignlanguage.com).

Motivation, participation and involvement

Some children are motivated only by certain software programs. These tend to combine the possibility of success for that particular child with a certain type of layout and screen content and rapid feedback style. To interest them in the Web site one then faces another access barrier: motivational access. Ideally, as we become more skilled at Web page making, we shall be able to design for these factors.

Children with autism may need a more structured approach at times, using worksheets or on-line activities such as the JavaScript mentioned earlier, and Web site sections incorporating their special interests and music. Some pupils have improved their reading through accessing the Christmas song sections and we have plans to incorporate common special interests such as transport, animals and buildings, with links to sites on television programmes and Disney films. For some children, working in a group of two or three, taking turns with the staff member asking questions, and relating the screen to their experience and know-ledge, help their concentration and participation. Some children will show more interest when given one-to-one help at the computer and others when given the computer to explore independently without direction.

Evaluation and the future

Children will become more familiar with using the school Web site and the Web in general as more parents go on-line. We shall then be working with parents to develop on-line activity sections useful at home. Our Web site continues to grow and develop, from seventeen pages in December 1998 to over 600 pages by June 2001. The plan for the future is to develop the Web site to integrate into all areas of school life, and to include more effective access to those children with additional disabili-ties. For all children the Web site will need to become more interactive. The development of a school intranet will enable materials to be shared on the network that we would not want to put on the Internet. Interactivity involving video, sound and larger file sizes may be more practical on an intranet, though this may change as we look forward to the introduction of broadband Internet services for schools. The key to further development is not only resources but staff training. As more appropriate subject materials become available on the Internet our Web site should be able to access them via links from areas where we investigate what those subject aspects mean for our children: a window on the world and a window on Mandeville School.

Summary

- Enable access for all children – investigate appropriate software, hardware, connection and design.
- Make the pages relevant to children and staff with frequent updates, reflecting whole-school events, reflecting individual needs, using photographs, with relevant external links and involving as much interactivity and multimedia as possible.
- When making the pages use enthusiasts, monitor ICT skill levels, have differentiated whole-school training, provide individual support, start with easy software first, and make reuseable pages.
- Integrate the Web site into the curriculum; provide in-class support and help with planning.

References

Abbott, C. (1998) *Making the Web Special*, London: King's College London and Institute of Education.

Abbott, C. (1999) *Making Communication Special*, London: King's College London.

Banes, D., and Walter, R. (2000) *Internet for All*, London: David Fulton.

De Cicco, E., Farmer, M., and Hargrave, C. (1999) *Activities for using the Internet in Primary Schools*, London: Kogan Page.

Miller, S., Larcher, J., and Robinson, P. (1999) 'Dynamic screen communication systems' I, *Communication Matters* 13 (3), 27–31.

TTA (1998) *National Standards for Qualified Teacher Status*, London: Teacher Training Agency

Chapter 4

The British Museum COMPASS Web site and learners with special needs

Carolyn Howitt and Jodi Mattes

In their description of the development of COMPASS (www. thebritishmuseum.ac.uk/compass), the inclusive Web site for the British Museum collections, Carolyn Howitt and Jodi Mattes demonstrate the importance of considering the needs of all users from the earliest stages of such a project.

COMPASS (COllections Multimedia Public AccesS System), featuring a selection of around 5,000 objects from the collections of the British Museum, has been live on the Web since June 2000. In 2002 it will also be accessible on specially designed touch screens in the refurbished Reading Room at the heart of the Museum's Great Court. Each object featured on COMPASS has a high-quality image, a 200-word article written by an expert, and links to background information and related objects. In combination these already make COMPASS a unique resource, but the Web site has been particularly praised for its ease of use and general accessibility.

From the start of the project we wanted to ensure that we produced a resource that could be used by as many people as possible. We particularly wanted to provide for specialist audiences who can often be excluded by Web technology, including visually impaired users or those with physical or learning disabilities. Accessibility issues can profoundly affect the content, design and navigation of a site: it is therefore not surprising that until recently a large proportion of sites have made little effort to appeal to those with specialist needs. Changing a site once it is live is far harder than integrating features from inception, so we decided to design for maximum accessibility right from the start.

There are many different kinds of disability, and it is not always helpful or realistic to divide those with special needs into distinct groups (Hardy

2000). Of course, the ideal Web site is one that is accessible to all, without making any group feel shut out. As a practical first step, we decided, it was necessary to define our target audiences and look at their specific needs. We realised that it was essential to involve the audience throughout in an on-going evaluation process, one that allowed time for changes to be implemented. We decided to look at the needs of visually impaired users on the Web during the initial design phase, then to provide additional tailored content for users with learning disabilities, both within and outside mainstream education.

Provision for visually impaired users

The first challenge was to plan a site that would be as accessible as possible to visually impaired and blind users. The COMPASS access co-ordinator, Jodi Mattes, researched various IT access organisations, such as AbilityNet, and disability organisations, such as the Royal National Institute for the Blind (RNIB). Also useful was *Making the Web Special*, a set of guidelines produced at King's College, London (Abbott 1998). Further guidelines for the production of accessible Web sites have since been published by the Web Accessibility Initiative (WAI 1999) and summarised by the RNIB (RNIB 2000).

The majority of people with visual impairments do have some sight, but may need Web pages that have been designed to be compatible with the specific access technology they are using. Some will benefit from magnification software that increases the size of information presented on the screen, while others use a screen reader with a speech synthesiser that reads aloud the text on the page. Different Web browsers include the facility to alter text size and colour, as well as background colour. This is of crucial importance to visually impaired users, many of whom have a preferred colour for viewing their pages most clearly. Some Web designers override this control in order to present a uniform appearance whatever the browser settings. It is crucial that flexibility is built into the design of the page, so that the individual can use the screen settings that suit them best.

One way of providing information that is compatible with screen-reading technology is to build a parallel text-only version of the Web site, where the screen reader can read off the text uninterrupted by images, icons and other insertions. Screen readers normally read across from top left to bottom right, so that text in columns will not be read correctly. The link to the text-only site needs to appear at the top left of the screen, where the screen reader will pick it up straight away. An exemplary site is

Figure 4.1 An example of a COMPASS screen

BBC Online, where text is frequently presented in columns on the graphical site, but on the parallel text-only site, using specially developed software known as Betsie (BBC Education Text to Speech Internet Enhancer), it is filtered to allow improved access to the site's content. Betsie also allows access to a high-contrast version, where text can be viewed in green on a black background. We decided to follow this model and build a text-only version of COMPASS, while still designing the graphical version to be as accessible as possible. The equivalent text-only page can be accessed from any page on the graphical site, and vice versa.

Frames pose the same difficulties as text in columns. A frame is the section of a screen that remains on a page (often forming a menu on the left-hand side) while the rest of the screen space changes. As a feature they can be extremely useful and are frequently used in Web design, but cannot be read by a screen reader reading from left to right. We decided not to use frames in the graphical version of COMPASS.

All images, icons and bitmap texts contain ALT text (alternative text). This usually appears in a small light yellow box when the cursor is moved over the object. The ALT text gives a brief description, explaining what can be seen in the image or the function of the icon. ALT text is read by screen readers, giving users access to more text information about potentially inaccessible images. The provision of ALT text for around

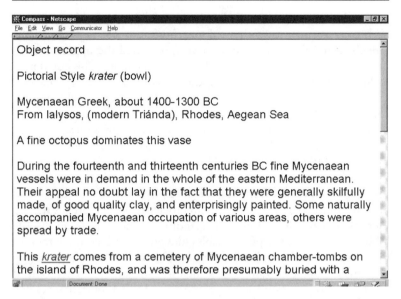

Figure 4.2 An example of a text alternative screen

7,000 images on COMPASS did become a larger, content development issue, and the decision was taken to generate it automatically using the relevant title and caption fields in the database.

Early on we had asked advice from the Sensory Disabilities Research Unit of the University of Hertfordshire. They also agreed to make a thorough evaluation of the Web site before it went live (University of Hertfordshire Sensory Disabilities Research Unit 2000). Ten people with visual impairments each completed a variety of tasks, including carrying out searches and looking for specific information. They then answered questions relating to the design of the site. Some completely blind users evaluated the text-only site, others the graphical version. They gave many useful suggestions on how to improve both the graphical and text-only sites. For example, since listening to synthesised speech can be monotonous, some information was moved higher up the page to make it more quickly accessible, and some links were removed. More minor problems included pop-up boxes, which could confuse the user (these were removed from the text-only version), and some of the options to alter text and colour which were not working across the whole page. Generally, however, the users were impressed with the ease of navigation of the site, and were delighted with the proposed provision, and that we had involved them at such an early stage.

For the future, it was clear from the evaluation that although blind Web users listening to synthesised speech want to reach information as quickly as possible, many would have appreciated the opportunity to hear further visual description of the images on display. This could have included details about the size, shape and colour of the object. One way of providing this could be through audio description in an additional narrative explanation of the museum object. In audio description of theatre or films, for example, body language, facial expression and scenery are all described so that someone with visual impairments is better informed of the bigger picture. This technique can be used to provide further description of objects (whether painting, sculpture or pottery) presented on museum Web sites. When displayed alongside background information, such detailed descriptions provide blind and partially sighted users with a much greater understanding of the objects on display. Web-based audio description enables museums and galleries to transfer the skills developed from live handling sessions on to Web and multimedia systems. Web-based technologies such as QuickTime, Synchronized Multimedia Integration Language (SMIL) and Synchronized Accessible Media Interchange (SAMI) can be used to provide audio description for visually impaired people as well as captioning for people with hearing difficulties. Museums such as the Finnish National Gallery and the National Museum of American History have developed on-line exhibitions that include longer description of images on display for users with visual impairments, provided as both text and live audio.

Provision for users with learning difficulties

A number of documents highlight museums' role in lifelong learning, including statements about access. *A Netful of Jewels: New Museums in the Learning Age* states specifically:

> The new technologies offer new ways for museums to work for social inclusion. Disabled people and others subject to barriers of distance or other factors will be able to benefit from museums' networked services.
>
> (Museum Directors' Conference 1999: 7)

There is no doubt that museums have a vital educational role to play within the community, and indeed, that this is an important responsibility. However accessible the COMPASS interface, we were aware that some audiences would benefit from specially written content. We were particularly anxious that adults and children with special learning needs were not left out of the planned provision.

It is extremely rare to find resources for learning disabled pupils on the Web unless they are part of a targeted special needs site like Becta's inclusion pages, part of the NGfL. Museums that put up worksheets to support visits tend to do this in PDF or other static formats aimed at one level of ability only, with the emphasis on the individual teacher to differentiate the work. Some museums, like London Transport Museum, offer resources specifically for students with special needs. As well as doing this, however, we also wanted students with learning difficulties to have access to the same content as other pupils. The Curriculum Inclusion Statement of the latest edition of the National Curriculum encourages teachers to:

> develop pupils' understanding through the use of all available senses and experiences, by using materials and resources that pupils can access through sight, touch, sound, taste or smell . . . using ICT, visual and other materials to increase pupils' knowledge of the wider world.
>
> (QCA 1999)

The structure of COMPASS lends itself well to the addition of content for specific audiences, particularly through its on-line Tours. COMPASS consists of two main elements: the Search facility, where the user can type in a term and retrieve related information, and Tours, specially authored selections of records that the user follows in a pre-set route. The Tours are ideal for the casual browser, those who are unsure about where to start, or for a specific audience. We have tours written for families, with two levels of information for adults and children, and tours written for children, either as a curriculum resource with accompanying worksheets or on topics of general interest such as 'Animal Mummies'.

As with the design of the COMPASS Web site, we felt that it was crucial to involve the target audience throughout in the development of this content. We enlisted the help of staff and pupils at Thurlow Park School in Lambeth, south London. The children at Thurlow Park have physical disabilities and associated language, communication and learning difficulties. Sadly, this excellent specialist school has now closed. The junior classes from Thurlow Park (twelve children in total) enjoyed horse riding regularly with the help of Riding for the Disabled. We decided to use the children's own experience of horses, in conjunction with depictions of horses and riders from ancient cultures on display in the British Museum, to produce supporting material for the National Curriculum for Art. The children were encouraged throughout to make careful observations and use a range of processes and materials.

The children first looked at some large posters in their art lesson, showing some of the many depictions of horses and riders in the Museum, and printed out from the COMPASS Web site. There was a general discussion about who the people were who were riding the horses, what the horses looked like, and how the artists had tried to show shape and texture. The children then did some preliminary sketches based on the pictures. The following week they visited the Museum, where they were delighted to see the objects they had got to know from the previous week's lesson, and, after a tour, completed some observational drawings. The highlight of the visit was the Parthenon touch wall, a copy of the famous frieze at wheelchair height, which enabled them to actually feel the horses' hoofs, manes and tails, and the position of the riders, and work out how they had been carved.

The following week was the highly successful Riding for the Disabled open day at Wimbledon Common, attended by all the junior children. Even those children who were not able to ride were encouraged to stroke the horses, feeling the different textures of their coats, manes and tails. Finally, back in the art room, the children produced some work in different media based on their experiences. These were then photographed with a digital camera and included in the on-line tour, next to COMPASS images of the museum objects, and alongside photographs of the children riding, working and in the Museum.

In order that the tour will continue to be useful to other schools in the future, we are producing a free teachers' pack, which includes lesson plans for the art lessons the children completed, cross-curricular resources to back up a visit to the Museum, and background information about the museum objects. It also contains a feedback sheet, so that we can monitor how the pack is being used, and how useful it continues to be. Ultimately we hope to author a complete area of COMPASS to support children and adults with learning difficulties. This would contain specially written simplified records about star objects from the Museum, and a few tours on popular subjects such as 'Animals' or 'Gold', along with puzzles and games aimed specifically at this group of users.

Within mainstream education

The vast majority of children with special needs are now educated within mainstream schools, and the current trend continues to be as inclusive as possible (Farrell 2001). A separate educational area of COMPASS will be launched, initially containing activities and resources aimed at children at Key Stage 2 and their teachers. These are mainly focused on the History topics from the National Curriculum, but also cover other subjects such as Literacy, Numeracy, Science and Art. We wanted to ensure that these were designed to be useful for a wide range of abilities within the classroom, including pupils with special educational needs. Allowing for differentiation is a real challenge facing on-line educational providers: often teachers have four or five different levels of ability within one class. This is particularly difficult when a Web site is aimed at a wide age range, such as an entire Key Stage, as is common. The COMPASS children's area is aimed at Key Stage 2, ages 8–11, but also includes some resources for Key Stages 1 and 3, so clearly much thought was required to ensure that as many pupils could access the information as possible.

As a first step, we contacted a number of local schools and talked to ICT co-ordinators, special needs co-ordinators, Heads and classroom teachers, with interesting results. We found that teachers were not as ICT-illiterate as is often reported: all of them used the Web in the staff room, to help find teaching resources, or at home. They all reported an increase in confidence with using on-line resources, due to recent training and updated equipment. However, they did not use the Web so much as a teaching tool in the classroom, except to teach specific ICT skills such as searching or information retrieval. This was partly due to lack of equipment, but also to lack of knowledge of useful sites. ICT was mainly used to help special needs children in specific areas, such as with literacy, rather than when studying other subjects, such as History, more broadly as a whole class. There seemed to be two main areas where special needs children particularly needed help in accessing information on COMPASS: first with the text and information on the actual Web site, and then with any activities linked to this, both on and off line, including worksheets and multimedia activities. We realised that any additional provision for special needs had to address both these areas, in order for children to get full use of the Web site.

Web site navigation and design

Once we had noted teachers' comments in our initial discussions, we built a grey-screen version of the education site for evaluation purposes. The screens had no design features, but included outlines of all planned content. The grey screens were produced very quickly and simply using

Netscape Composer, and provided an on-screen way of demonstrating the functionality of the site, including all links. When completed, they were sent out to schools and some LEA advisers for their comments, followed up by visits where questionnaires were filled in. One of the areas we asked about was the proposed provision for special needs pupils, and a number of schools mentioned how useful they would find it if the on-screen text could somehow be read out loud. Although this will not be included until Phase II of the project, so far it has led us to look into screen-reading software such as the free Speaks for Itself plug-in. Once downloaded, the software reads out any text on the page that it has been programmed to, including icons and buttons, ensuring that the same content is accessible to all children in a class, whatever their reading level.

Activities and paper resources

It was necessary to make an early decision about how to make worksheets and paper resources useful for as many abilities as possible. However, we did not want teachers to have to print a vast number of worksheets, each for a slightly different ability group. As well as confusing, this could also be seen as patronising, as teachers clearly know best how to differentiate work for their own pupils. There are also so many levels of ability within one class that in order to cater for many different pupils a huge number of worksheet variations would be needed. However, discussions with teachers equally showed that overwhelmingly they are short of time, so are grateful for any ready-made resource that can be quickly printed, particularly if they know it has been tried and tested with a class of the relevant age group.

One way of dealing with this apparent conflict is to provide resources in a format that teachers can download and alter quickly for their particular class. The challenge here is to make it simple to do, as many teachers are just beginning to use the Web, and downloading and altering documents can seem daunting at first. There is also the technical problem of ensuring that whatever format is used is compatible with software used by teachers, as well as providing a version of the document that looks the same no matter which browser is used. Traditionally, documents for printing from the Web are in PDF format, viewed through an Adobe Acrobat Reader, which has the advantage of being free to download and quick and easy to use. However, documents viewed in this way cannot be altered, and so, although we considered having puzzles and colouring sheets attached in this format, we realised that it did not lend itself to worksheets to use as educational tools with a whole class. We also discussed the possibility of using HTML documents, though these can alter in appearance depending on the browser used, and would still need to be downloaded in order to be amended for different abilities. We eventually decided to use Word Viewer to view attached files, as it displays the document in exactly the same way that it has been created, but it can also be downloaded and altered easily on the user's machine using Microsoft Word. Word Viewer can even be used without Word; it has the added advantage of being free and fast to download from the Web.

Worksheets are attached to COMPASS tours on specific subjects of the curriculum. From any screen the teacher clicks on Teaching Resources, and is taken to a page with a number of teaching suggestions and a link to a worksheet. All teaching suggestions include how to differentiate the activity for more and less able pupils.

Before each Tour is launched, it will be tested in the classroom by a local school studying that topic. Time for amendments is built into the planning process. Once a Tour has been live for a while, a further qualitative evaluation will be planned, in addition to the usual quantitative assessment of site visit statistics. One of the Tour features is the facility to display children's work, as well as including a link to a school Web site if it contains relevant material. One of the benefits of the Web as a medium is the ability to keep the information fresh and continually updated, but this needs organisation and staff resources to ensure it happens on a regular basis.

The personal folder feature being developed for COMPASS is of particular use to classroom teachers. It will enable a teacher to save individual COMPASS articles into an on-line folder, protected with a password, which they or their class can re-access later to explore in more detail, either from home or in the classroom. Objects within folders can be moved and sorted according to material, date and so on. There are a number of sub-folders, ensuring that different selections can be saved for different ability or interest groups.

The provision for special needs that COMPASS has so far managed to produce for a variety of audiences has been time-consuming. This has partly been due to the lack of guidelines and relevant examples of good practice, but the situation is changing. We believe that soon all major Web sites will plan from the start to be fully accessible as a matter of course, rather as access for people with physical disabilities to new buildings is now a legal requirement (Disability Discrimination Act 1995). However, we are also aware that there are many other specialist audiences which COMPASS could yet cater for, and which we hope to provide for in the future, including those in mainstream and special secondary education. As well as the continual involvement of the target audience, we could not have achieved as much as we have without planning the provision in a fully integrated manner into the project as a whole. This was possible only with the continual support and involvement of the rest of the COMPASS team, as well as our software suppliers.

Summary

- Resource developers and content owners, such as museums, should aim to make their Web sites accessible to as wide a range of users as possible.
- There are particular needs related to people with visual impairment, and screen design and functionality can do much to assist this group.
- Parallel text-only sites can be an effective addition to an inclusive Web site.
- Many of the disability organisations can offer valuable advice on accessibility and the Web.
- There is no replacement for significant piloting of a new resource with real users.
- A number of issues need to be considered before making paper or downloadable resources available.
- The development of an accessible Web site is a team enterprise.

References

Abbott, C. (1998) *Making the Web Special*, London: King's College London and Institute of Education.

Farrell, P. (2001) 'Special education in the last twenty years: have things really got better?' *British Journal of Special Education* 28(1): 3–9.

Hardy, C. (2000) *Information and Communications Technology for All*, London: David Fulton.

Museum Directors' Conference (1999) *A Netful of Jewels: New Museums in the Learning Age*, London: Museum Directors' Conference.

QCA (1999) Curriculum Inclusion Statement, UK National Curriculum, www.nc.uk.net/inclusion.html (accessed 1 June 2001).

Royal National Institute for the Blind (2000) *Hints for Designing Accessible Web Sites*, available on-line at www.rnib.org.uk/digital/hints.htm (accessed 1 June 2001).

University of Hertfordshire Sensory Disabilities Research Unit (2000) 'An Evaluation of the British Museum COMPASS Web site with Visually Impaired People' (unpublished).

Web Accessibility Initiative (1999) *Web Content Accessibility Guidelines*, www. w3.org/WAI/Resources/#gl (accessed 1 June 2001).

Web links

AbilityNet   www.abilitynet.co.uk
Royal National Institute for the Blind   www.rnib.org.uk
BBC Online   www.bbc.co.uk
BBC Education Text to Speech Internet Enhancer   www.bbc.co.uk/
  education/betsie/about.html
Finnish National Gallery   www.fng.fi/fng/html4/en/default.htm
National Museum of American History   www.americanhistory.si.edu/
  disabilityrights/welcome.html
BECTA's National Grid for Learning Inclusion site   inclusion.ngfl.gov.uk
London Transport Museum   www.ltmuseum.co.uk/education/maing.
  html
National Curriculum Online, inclusion statement   www.nc.uk.net/
  inclusion.html
Riding for the Disabled   www.riding-for-disabled.org.uk/main.htm
Speaks for Itself   www.speaksforitself.com

Acknowledgements

System Simulation Ltd www.ssl.co.uk
University of Hertfordshire, Sensory Disabilities Research Unit
phoenix.herts.ac.uk/SDRU/hmpage.html
Thurlow Park Special School

Sadly, Jodi Mattes died in December 2001, aged only 28, before this
book was published. Jodi was passionately dedicated to making the web
accessible, and her work in this field has been a huge inspiration to her
colleagues. We are committed to ensuring that Jodi's work is continued
after her death.

Chapter 5

Inclusion and the Web
Strategies for improving access

Sally Paveley

> In her dual role as a teacher and teacher educator Sally Paveley
> discusses the various ways in which young people with learning
> difficulties can be helped to access the World Wide Web and explains
> the strategies she has developed.

The powerful potential of the Internet is unfolding around us as we
learn more about its use as a tool to support teaching and learning.
Government funding has ensured that what began a decade ago as a
vision shared by a few has entered the mainstream consciousness of the
teaching profession. However, the concept of the Internet as 'a means
through which we can participate and contribute to a society in which
learning is increasingly accessible and adapted to individual needs' (Blair
2001) has still not been fully realised, either for students who have severe
learning difficulties or the teachers who support them.

The potential importance of the Internet to students who have severe
learning difficulties is illustrated in this message, posted to a self-advocacy
mailing list:

> The Internet is the most revolutionary technology ever for people
> with learning difficulties. We must work to teach people that access
> for people with learning difficulties is a basic right. If we don't we
> will be left out.

> (Usupport 1998)

This chapter will look at practical ways in which this group of students
can be given access to the part of the Internet known as the World Wide
Web.

Setting the scene

In the early 1990s students from George Hastwell School, Cumbria, used e-mail to communicate with a school in Canada. The possibility of using the Internet to extend the learning experiences of students with severe learning difficulties was established at around this time. Although there followed a period during which development was slow, the arrival of the World Wide Web saw the Internet blossom into the multimedia communications tool we use today.

The World Wide Web is potentially an ideal medium for presenting information to students who have severe learning difficulties because, in addition to text, it can be used to display pictures and to play animations, sound and video clips. Yet much of the Web is not accessible because the content is too complex for these students to understand. Web sites designed for young children are sometimes cognitively suitable but inappropriate for older students. Even Web sites that are designed for educational use are often beyond the grasp of students who have severe learning difficulties. Similarly search engines require a level of literacy that is beyond the ability of most students with severe learning difficulties.

Adapting media that are intended for more able learners is a task undertaken frequently by teachers in this sector of education. More suitable Web content will come on-line as time passes; meanwhile it is necessary to find ways to adapt Web resources that are currently available.

I have been teaching ICT to a group of secondary-age students who have severe learning difficulties at Rosemary School, Islington. Part of the work has involved students using the Web for a variety of purposes, and this work will provide case studies to illustrate ideas in this chapter. In my role as a trainer I have also discussed the use of the Web with a wider audience of teachers during training courses and at a conference on the Internet. Points raised during these discussions will also be presented.

Introducing the Internet

Explaining the World Wide Web to anybody who is not familiar with ICT is a challenge; it is an even more complex task if you are teaching students with severe learning difficulties. The language of the Internet is penetrating society as more and more families use it. A number of students I have worked with are familiar with Internet terminology even if they are not really sure what it means. Many students with severe

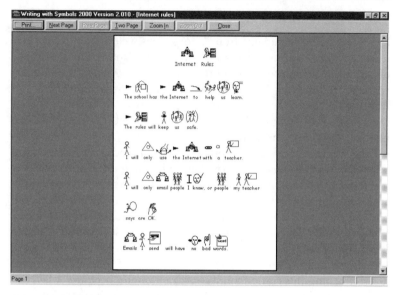

Figure 5.1 Internet rules

learning difficulties are also aware that the Web and e-mail have something to do with computers, but they can learn about the Internet only through using it and finding out what it can do.

Schools are required to ensure that students follow a set of rules when they use the Internet. This applies to all schools, including special schools. The students at Rosemary School have been given a set of rules written in symbol-enhanced text using clear and straightforward language, and the students went through these rules at regular intervals to ensure that they became familiar with them.

Accessing the Web

Most people who use the Web do so by using a mouse. They learn quickly which buttons to click, how to surf from page to page by clicking on linked text and pictures, and how to use the browser tools such as the Back button and the Favorites list. For many students with severe learning difficulties a mouse is not easy to control, and the browser tools will take time to learn. Physical access may be an issue. This was the case for a number of the Rosemary School students when they were first introduced to the Web. A group of sixth-form students began to explore Web resources with the help of a classroom assistant who used search engines to locate topics in which the students expressed an interest. The students became engaged in the activity when suitable Web sites were located, but soon became bored and lost concentration while the searches were taking place. There was a clear need for a quick and easy way to get to interesting Web sites.

One possible solution was to put Web sites into the list of Favorites but most of the students were not able to read the items in this. Instead, direct links to Web sites were created on an overlay keyboard and this was used as an alternative to the Favorites list. Graphics from the Web sites that the students could easily understand were copied on to the paper overlay so all the students had to do was press a picture, for example, of the *EastEnders* logo, and they would then go direct to the *EastEnders* home page. Once they had reached the home page the students were encouraged to use the mouse to explore the site, and this they managed with varying degrees of success. Importantly, the students remained in control, they could always go back to the home page or to another site, and the level of frustration was much reduced.

This idea was developed further when some students wanted to explore a particular site. They wanted to be able to find and print photographs of singers in a pop band. This time an overlay that contained links into particular Web pages within the site was created. The overlay also contained tools such as the arrow keys for scrolling up and down a page and a Print button so they could print pages independently. The students were asked to seek permission before printing. This overlay proved very popular and students would often ask to use it.

Access using an intranet

An intranet is a closed network accessible to a restricted number of people. Many schools and colleges set up their own intranets, containing information that is relevant to them and links to Web sites that will support the curriculum they teach. An intranet has been developed for the staff and students at Rosemary School. The intranet contains an area with Web links for the staff to use and an area that some of the students are able to use independently.

The idea for the design of the students' area came from the work with the overlay keyboard. The menu page contains pictorial links to pages that have links to Web sites in a particular category, such as sport, music, animals or television. This works well for some of the more able students who have good mouse control and are able to use the Back and Home buttons on the browser. The advantage of the intranet over using

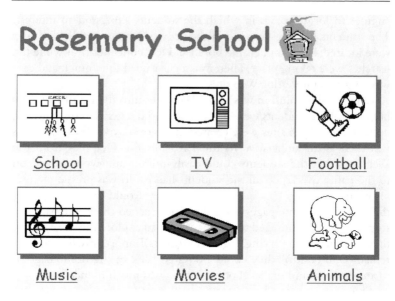

Figure 5.2 The Rosemary School intranet

an overlay keyboard is that a greater number of sites can be made available but a simple layout can be retained: this is because the sites are nested within categories. The Home button always returns the user to the first page in the intranet so students cannot get lost.

One student who was able to access the Internet in this way said that he wanted to know what was written on the Web pages. He was not able to read well enough to make sense of the text but TextHelp, a program that reads any text that is highlighted, was installed on the computer, and he was shown how to use it. He was delighted because he could investigate Web sites more fully and do so independently. The language used on some sites was too complex for him to comprehend but that has not dampened his enthusiasm.

Access using switches

Providing access to the Web for students who have a physical disability in addition to a learning difficulty is an even greater challenge. Richard Walter, ICT co-ordinator at Meldreth Manor School, has pioneered work in this area. He has worked with students in his school to develop a Web site that is accessible to switch users, and has written a detailed account of how it was done (Banes and Walter 2000). Richard's students have been involved in a host of practical activities designed to enhance their understanding of the Web. These include cutting up photographs then posting them down big paper tubes and reassembling them, an activity designed to illustrate the way in which information is transmitted by the Internet. His students have also been involved in choosing photographs to put on the Meldreth Manor School site (www. meldrethmanor.com).

Richard has used a very simple and extremely effective idea to make the students' pages on the Meldreth Manor Web site accessible to switch users. He has put a button in the same place in the top right corner of every page. This button is a hyperlink to the next page, and the teacher places the mouse pointer on it. The switches are connected to the computer via a mouse; when the switch is pressed the computer responds as if a mouse button has been pressed and activates the link to the next page.

There are some utility programs that can be used to provide switch access to Web sites. Switch access utilities designed to provide access to computers for people who have a physical disability can be used, but these are generally too cognitively demanding for students with severe or profound and multiple learning difficulties (SLD/PMLD). Programs that allow switch-accessible hot spots to be created on the screen could also be used. These are most effective if the Web page layouts are consistent, and the challenge then is to find Web sites designed with the needs of such users in mind.

Making use of the Web

Much of the early work on the Web with the students at Rosemary School was exploratory. The students were learning about the Web by exploring Web sites, or surfing, as it has become known. A later project involved the students in being more purposeful in their use of the Web. The students were creating multimedia presentations about themselves and they used the Web to find pictures to illustrate their presentations. For example, one student said that Ronan Keating was her favourite pop star, so we found photographs of him and she chose the one she wanted to put into her presentation. The photograph was then copied and pasted into the multimedia software. Similarly, when the students were working on a newspaper, they used the Web to find photographs to illustrate some of their articles. Unsurprisingly, this group of students is now confident that a picture of almost anything can be found on the Web if it is needed.

Other teachers in the school have also used the Web to find and print resources to support their teaching. One good example of such a resource is the Egyptian section on the British Museum's Web site (www.thebritishmuseum.ac.uk/compass/). There are lots of pictures of Egyptian artefacts and even stories about life in ancient Egypt. One teacher has been using the Web to get maps of towns for a Geography topic; another has found an interactive maths Web site and her pupils have used it to explore mazes. A data projector could really bring such resources to life for students; connected to a computer, a data projector would enable teachers to display such resources on a large screen or interactive whiteboard so that whole groups could discuss them and interact with them.

Teachers who plan to use a Web site as part of a lesson do need to check that it is available before the lesson begins, and that the Internet connection is working properly. The Web is an ever-changing phenomenon and some organisations seem to change both the content and the location of their Web site just when you want to use it. It is possible to download pages from a Web site and use them off-line, although you need special software to do so and you need to be selective about what you download because some Web sites are too big to be downloaded in their entirety.

Similarly, if you plan to use a Web site that has multimedia resources such as sound clips and video, you do need to ensure that the computer you will be using has the required plug-ins loaded. These are little programs, usually free to download, that you need to have installed on your computer before music and video will work. The best way to check is to try out the site on the computer you plan to use and see if it works.

Issues

The main focus of our work on the Web at Rosemary School has been concerned with finding and printing or copying pictures. Through this the students have learned a number of things about the Web, including that it is a source of information, that you can click on links to go to different pages and that you can click the Home button or press an overlay to return to a familiar page. They have also learned that you can print information and put pictures into other programs.

The Web is not a readily accessible resource for students who have severe learning difficulties and teachers do need to use their ICT skills and imagination to make it more accessible. A growing number of Web sites now offer alternative text-only areas for people who have a visual impairment and need to use a screen reader. There is mounting pressure from groups such as the self-advocacy movement for Web sites to be made more accessible for people with learning difficulties. There should also be pressure from those of us in education for educational Web sites to be made more accessible. For example, educational Web designers could be encouraged to include an alternative area that has a simplified version of the information with a clear, consistent layout and a voice to read out any text.

Interactive multimedia sites that make the Web come to life are a potentially exciting and valuable resource. However, teachers at Rosemary School have found interactive Web sites to be either cognitively suitable but designed for pre-school children or requiring the user to read instructions and perform tasks which are too complex. These are both barriers to the students. Another difficulty with interactive Web sites is the requirement for many plug-ins to be downloaded before the activity can be used. Perhaps we need to wait for the next generation of Web technology before such resources become easy to use.

As the resources on the Web expand there is a growing need for a quick way for teachers to access information about suitable Web sites. They could do so by sharing their discoveries, and mailing lists such as the SLD Forum do allow teachers to share information but are not really suitable for this particular purpose. There are educational Internet service providers who make up-to-date information about suitable curricular Web resources available to their subscribers in mainstream schools. A similar service for teachers in SLD schools would be a very useful tool.

There is no doubt that the Web, in common with other services provided by the Internet, is an integral feature of teaching and learning – not just the teaching and learning that will take place in the future but that which is taking place now. Students who have severe learning difficulties share the same entitlement to its potential benefits as all other students. While there are a number of obstacles that stand in the way of that entitlement, there are tools that can help students to overcome these while we wait for more general improvements in accessibility. The challenge is for teachers to use such tools skilfully and imaginatively.

There is a greater challenge to those who determine educational policy and to those who supply educational Web resources. This challenge is to ensure that access to the Web is improved over the long term so that teachers and students have the resources they need without having to make adaptations. We must ensure that students who have severe learning difficulties are not disadvantaged, or bypassed, as ideas, initiatives and resources progress. The Web and what it can offer is too important for that.

Summary

- The Web is not yet as accessible as it needs to be.
- Students with learning difficulties are often unable to use standard Web tools such as search engines.
- Students with learning difficulties need to understand something about the Internet as well as how to use it.
- All students need to follow good practice guidelines when using the Internet.
- Peripherals such as switches and overlay keyboards can help some students access the Internet.
- A school intranet can offer alternative access methods to the Internet.
- Web resources can be useful to teachers in SLD schools as well as to students.
- Cognitive accessibility is a problem with some Web sites.
- Short-term solutions can be created by ingenious teachers, but policy change is needed to ensure that the Web remains accessible to all.

References

Banes, D., and Walter, R. (2000) *Internet for All*, London: David Fulton.

Blair, T. (2001) *National Grid for Learning* foreword, available at on-line www. dfee.gov.uk/grid/challenge/foreword.htm (accessed on 20 May 2001).

Usupport (1998) Message posted to the Usupport Mailing List, Central England People First, www.peoplefirst.org.uk (accessed in May 1998).

Part II

Communicating with others

Chapter 6

Making communication special

Chris Abbott

Communication is a basic human right, and the Internet offers new opportunities for extending that right to previously disadvantaged groups. Alongside opportunities come risks, and those responsible for communication projects must be aware of these.

The use of e-mail within curriculum projects has become well established in the UK and many other countries. The medium provides speedy access, a sense of urgency and feedback which is almost immediate, provided that all the partners involved recognise these as aims to be pursued. Teachers working with students with special educational needs (SEN) have found there are particular benefits for these young learners.

That it isn't their school is very significant for them; and that these children that write to them or fax to them aren't here. They've got no concept of where they live but they know the other children aren't in their school, they are somewhere outside of it and that's very, very important conceptually, and it has helped us to reinforce that very basic concept: there's something larger than me . . .
(A special school teacher in e-mail to the author, June 2000)

Why communicate with other schools?

For too long, and on far too many occasions, young people with special educational needs have been isolated from their peers. Whether they are in physically separate provision, often in the form of special schools in isolated country locations, or nominally included in a school which has not yet managed to make that inclusion a reality, their communicative needs continue to be a cause of concern for many.

All young people in our schools, whatever their particular need, have the right to be heard: information and communications technology (ICT) together with the Internet can greatly increase the number of opportunities for this to happen. The right to communicate has been well expressed in an important statement by the American Speech–Language–Hearing Association (ASHA 1992). This statement, described as a Communication Bill of Rights, was devised by the National Joint Committee for the Communication Needs of Persons with Severe Disabilities, a US group.

The Communication Bill of Rights asserts the right of all persons, 'regardless of the extent or severity of their disabilities'. It talks about the right to request things or make choices, the right to decline and the right to request feedback. It goes on to cover the right to interaction with others, the right to information and, importantly, the right of access to alternative and augmentative communication (AAC) devices. Further rights deal with the environmental, cultural and linguistic contexts, as well as the need to ensure the essential dignity which is also a right. The full statement (ASHA 1992) is an eloquent summary which deserves to be widely known and to serve as an aim for all who work in this area.

Although the Communication Bill of Rights was drafted with the needs of persons with severe disabilities in mind, many of its demands are equally relevant to young people with a wider variety of special educational needs. Too often, students in schools for the emotionally and behaviourally disturbed (EBD), for example, are extremely isolated from their peers.

Meldreth Manor (http://www.meldrethmanor.com) is a residential school for pupils with cerebral palsy and severe or profound learning difficulties. The school uses ICT frequently and teachers there have written (Banes and Walter 2000) about the ways in which they have explained the Internet to students, and Sally Paveley described in the last chapter how the school has made the Internet explicable to students. Its model of the transmission of messages on the Internet, made more realistic by using the recorded sounds of a modem, was operated by students using switches. The model was then developed further to introduce the ideas of addresses and of congestion on the network. The series of activities introduced the students to the basic concepts of transmitting data, always based on their own experiences and understanding.

Although the Internet has been available for many years now, it is only quite recently that its use in schools has become widespread. Now that most schools have Internet access, at least in some areas, it is becoming more and more difficult for institutions to function without this facility. The arrival of resources from the DfES Standards Fund has provided levels of access in many special schools and special needs settings which would have been unthinkable a few years ago. All teachers have also been offered training under the New Opportunities Fund (NOF) scheme, and this has been available from specialists in the SEN area.

The hidden potential of the fax

Electronic communication does not have to involve the Internet, of course, and it is easy to forget the power of the written letter or the directness of a telephone call. Perhaps the most accessible of the technologies that most schools already have available is the fax machine.

Fax is immediate and costs are much lower than if the same amount of information were to be spoken during a phone call. It is not, however, as cheap as the Internet, where information travels much more quickly and where all calls are at local rate. Some schools manage to reduce costs by using a fax with the option of storing a message and transmitting it overnight when costs are lower, but to do this is to lose some of the immediacy of the process as well as the potential for getting a reply fairly quickly, before the students have forgotten all about sending the message.

At Elleray Park School, near Liverpool, fax messaging has been used by students with a wide range of severe learning difficulties. Some students can walk but many others are wheelchair users. Elleray Park has been using fax in the curriculum for several years and now has three fax machines, thanks to its involvement in the BT Faxbuddies project. Much of the communication in the school uses Rebus symbols, often through the use of Writing with Symbols 2000 (Widgit Software). The availability of three fax machines makes it possible for one class to fax another, often using the school's bank of symbols, developed by the language co-ordinator, who is also a speech therapist. Control technology is used to give the students access to the Literacy Hour.

Standards Fund resourcing means that the school now has a mini-network with Internet access, but Elleray Park still sees a real future in the use of fax for communication, and uses the technology to help students develop a sense of place, and to help them progress from interpreting symbols to developing a concept of self. For this reason, the school would like to have access to a fax machine with photograph buttons linked to a digital memory, so that students could press the image of the person they wished to fax. It is possible that the rapid increase of fax services on the Internet will make this possible.

There are conceptual problems with the use of fax for some people with learning difficulties. One school described the process of introducing a class to fax for the first time by writing a message in symbols and reminding the students about their previous experience of writing a letter home. All the students had done this, writing a message in symbols for their parents, taking it to a post-box and posting it, and then later seeing it arrive at home. When it came to sending the fax the teacher explained that it was just like posting a letter in a box but that this time it would be sent immediately. Of course, what the students saw was a letter going into a machine and then immediately coming out again: this made one of them suggest, quite logically, that the fax was not working. A school with only one fax will find it very difficult to explain the process, but having a second machine could make all the difference, even if it is only one borrowed for a short while from elsewhere.

It is also worth while trying to afford a fax machine which uses plain paper rather than the curly, shiny type which does not last. A memory for numbers is useful, as is the ability to send at different speeds so that symbols can be sent quickly and cheaply but photographs more slowly in order to keep as much of the image detail as possible. Effective fax messages can also be very simple – a few symbols on a page can lead to a quick response where several sentences might be too daunting for the users at the other end. Several schools have also found it valuable to send short video clips through the post so that each class can see and hear their partners. Video is a very immediate medium, and students responded quickly and enthusiastically to this, so that they were very eager to begin sending faxes to the people they had seen on screen.

Planning effective e-mail projects

Perhaps the most widely known facility offered by the Internet is the ability to send and receive electronic mail. There are many ways of helping young people do this. To start with, many schools find that one school address is sufficient, with all messages going through this account and the teacher receiving the replies and passing them on to students. Quite quickly, however, most schools decide to move to some form of multiple addresses – perhaps one address per class or, in some cases, one for each student. Many schools subscribe to an Internet Service Provider (ISP) which provides multiple e-mail addresses, but others use Web-based mail services. These are essentially free, since they are paid for by the advertising which appears on screen when mail is sent or received. Whether this is acceptable in an educational context is a matter for discussion within the school, and it is important that an agreed policy develops which is understood by staff and parents. In some cases, advertising can be offensive as well as intrusive, depending on the goods and services in question. In any case, the move to individual e-mail addresses must be accompanied by agreement on how they are to be managed. Older students who are able to understand the issues involved should be asked to sign an agreement on how the facility will be used; in all other cases, parental permission should be sought. Schools would not, after all, issue every student with a mobile telephone without getting parental permission and deciding on acceptable use; in many ways, access to e-mail is a similar issue.

E-mail projects work best when some of the teachers involved have already met each other, as is clear from David Ware in Chapter 7 about his school's experience with Netlinks. It becomes so much easier to come to agreement quickly, to understand what the other educator is trying to gain from the process, and, crucially, to know someone well enough to say no when a plan clearly is not right for one of the partners. All e-mail projects should have end dates, and some of the best projects last for a very short time. Two weeks seems about right: enough time for three or four exchanges of information and yet not too long so that boredom sets in. Of course, if the experience is a successful one, there is no reason why a further project might not follow at a later date between the same partner classes.

David Fettes wrote in Chapter 3 about the school's experience of developing a Web site, but Mandeville has also experimented with e-mailing symbols, even before the add-on program was developed to make this easy. The school tried e-mailing a similar school which also used the Writing with Symbols program. The first problem was to find a partner class using the same symbol set: Mandeville uses Makaton symbols mostly but the partner school used Rebus. The next difficulty was caused by the adaptability of the program: each user can create new word lists and new symbols – but if the files are then e-mailed those symbols may not exist in the partner school. After some discussion, the problem was solved by sending plain text files which could then appear in each school with the locally used symbols.

Many schools get involved in educational and community on-line projects which provide a ready source of potential partners. Netlinks (http://www.suhsd.k12.ca.us/mvm/netlinks/contents.html) has already been mentioned, but others include iEarn (http://www.iearn.org/) and

Computer Pals across the World (http://reach.ucf.edu/~cpaw/index.
html). Many educational ISPs such as RM Learning Alive (http://www.
learningalive.co.uk/) also provide a place for potential education partners
to meet. Perhaps the best beginning, however, is a face-to-face meeting
between two teachers at a conference or other event followed by the
decision to link their classes.

Travel Buddies is an excellent project originally set up by the British
Council in Australia; each class sends a cuddly toy to the other country.
The toys are then taken on trips, diaries are written for them and
photographs taken before they are sent home – sometimes a little the
worse for wear. David Ware explains in Chapter 7 how it works, and his
school's Travel Buddy, Spike, is now a veteran of many trips. Closed pen-
pal groups can be a good idea, too, especially as a way of linking together
users who communicate in the same way. Schools with large numbers
of symbol users may find it helpful to join the symbol users' mailing list
operated by Widgit Software – full details are available on their Web site
(www.widgit.com).

Using on-line chat

One of the earliest facilities added to the Internet was the abilty to chat
by typing on screen, in real time, with someone else also connected
at that moment. The most well known way of doing this was by use of
Internet Relay Chat (IRC), but more recently an enormous range
of chat environments has appeared on the Web, either as part of services
like Yahoo or on individual users' home pages.

Often seen as the Wild West of the Internet, chat is in many ways
a wholly inappropriate place for schools to consider using. It is easy for
users to preserve their anonymity, at least from other users if not from
the authorities. Chat is usually unmoderated and uncensored and it is
very easy to send pictures as well as text to the person involved. In most
cases, open-access chat will not be appropriate for school use at all.

Researchers, on the other hand, have found chat to be a fertile
environment for tracing the socio-linguistic practices of Internet users,
as well as the textual changes that appear to be part of the phenomenon.
Discussions in the popular press of the use of contractions and acronyms
when sending text message by mobile phone have many similarities to
previous discussion of similar practices in on-line chat rooms, or even as
part of previous technologies such as citizen band radio (CB) in the
1960s or even short-wave radio in the 1950s (Abbott 2000). Researchers
who have published in this area have tended to do so in edited collections

(Dery 1994; Jones 1997; Strate *et al.* 1996) which have focused on a few well known incidents and have usually been related to the activities of university students. The on-line practices of school-age students, whether they have special educational needs or not, are far less well researched and are certainly worthy of greater attention.

Some researchers and writers have focused in particular on the mechanisms by which the Internet can assist in the formation of identity and self-esteem. Turkle in particular, who does discuss young people (Turkle 1984, 1996), raises many issues which are relevant to students with SEN who may feel less included than they should be in mainstream education. The notion that identity is of vital importance to students with disability in particular is underlined by another published work, this time located within a special school in the UK (Nicholls 1997). In his discussion of the role that the creation of artworks plays in his students' developing understanding of their place in the world, Nicholls indicates the particular role that ICT can play. His personal philosophy of teaching bears repeating here, since it indicates something of the potential of on-line activity.

> ideally we teach in an atmosphere of trust, so engendering self-belief and self-esteem and even, in a sense, love of the self. . . . As creative human beings we constantly interrogate ourselves in relation to the world. . . . In art, and in the evolution of spiritual revelation, and in the revelation of scientific revolution, we mirror nature.
>
> (Nicholls 1997: 45–6)

Online chat, banal though much of it may be, is an attempt to mirror nature, to provide a mechanism to 'stand for' human speech in geographical proximity. Although his book antedates his use of the Internet, Nicholls has gone on to develop his work through on-line projects, and his was the special education partner school for the British Museum project described in Chapter 4.

Some schools have developed ways of using chat productively and safely. Springwell Dene in Sunderland is a school for children with emotional and behavioural difficulties. Teachers at the school are aware of the real difficulties that many of their students have with social relations and they feel that on-line chat offers an environment in which they can learn how to deal with this area. Filtering software on the school network makes it impossible for offensive words or descriptions to appear onscreen, whether typed by the school student or by the respondent. Students have been taught to break off the conversation if it appears that the topic is not appropriate, and images cannot be sent or received. The school monitors and logs all conversations, and the students are aware of this.

One student with severe communication difficulties likes chatting on IRC because he can take time to respond and can ask staff what is meant by the people he is talking to. Another student has problems with spelling but does not like others to know this: on IRC he has time to check spellings before he sends each comment. School staff monitor IRC conversations and use them as teaching opportunities for discussing what is and is not acceptable in conversation. Other students have shown remarkable reading gains after using IRC, with one girl also achieving much improved GCSE results after her confidence and communicative skills were improved in this way. Aggressive students, some affected by Ritalin and other drug therapies, have learnt to be patient, and to contribute in turn to conversation, through on-line chat.

The school has even begun to receive e-mails from ex-pupils.

> Hi there Mr Stafford well bet you would not expect this mail from me.
>
> So how r u doing I saw the school in the paper something about the conference and the school doing live broadcast. I also saw about Mr [*name removed*]'s son, tell him I send my regards and hope he gets better soon, say hi to all the staff for me . . . if you want to e-mail me back I'm [*address removed*]
>
> P.S. I guess I should let you know this is Tom.
>
> (E-mail from 20 year old ex-student of EBD school sent from his further education college)

Chat is developing fast, and some of the newer systems use the spoken voice rather than typed text; it will be much more difficult to regulate such an environment. However, as with typed text, the ability to link directly with one other known user is a much safer and more appropriate option than going to a public gathering point on the Internet and chatting with whomever may be found there.

Point-to-point communication is not an option when a school first begins, however, if no partner yet exists. One option here might be the use of a closed and password-protected chat area designed for educational use. There are many of these available but some are better designed than others. In general, the quicker it is to register and get access, the more teachers should be concerned about how protected the service may be. It should not be possible for users to chat anonymously, and the most protected services actually mail out passwords by post in order to ensure that a school is really just that and has given a valid address. Of course, this kind of service will need to charge a fee if only to cover its costs.

Using pictures: digital cameras

Many schools now have digital cameras, as these have been available for several years. They are now cheaper, lighter and easier to use. It is no longer necessary, in many cases, to connect the camera to the computer and download the images created; the files are saved immediately to a disc in the camera which can be removed and placed in the computer. Images, especially of students themselves, are an extremely powerful resource. Many schools with symbol users have added digital photographs to the symbol banks so that these appear when a student's name is typed, or the name appears when the image is selected.

The greater resolution offered by present-day fax machines enables photographic images to be sent as well as words and symbols. Since fax is a monochrome medium, black-and-white photographs work much better than colour, and if they can be converted to a lower definition dot-screened version first they will be much more effective. This used to be done by photocopying the image while it is covered with a dot screen but some software can do the same thing electronically. The highest resolution should always be selected on the fax when sending images; many Internet-connected computers can send such faxes at a higher quality than do dedicated fax machines.

Be aware at all times of the issues involved in the publication of images of students. This is just as important when using e-mail as it is during the development of a Web site. Sending a photograph to an e-mail partner, just as in attaching such an image to a home page, is an act of publication. As we would expect to get parental permission to publish a child's photograph in a book, so we should seek such permission to publish electronically.

It would be very constraining on the curriculum if permission were to be sought each time a new activity began; a much better solution is an agreed school policy on electronic images of students which is published in the school brochure and to which parents are asked to agree when students join the school. This policy might include the promise never to attach surnames to photographs, or that names will not be linked to particular photographs; the precise policy will vary according to the needs of students in that school and may also vary according to the age and developmental abilities of the students involved. The policy will also need regular updates as new possibilities open up in on-line publishing practices.

Summary

- Communication is a basic human right for all.
- Many young people with SEN have not had full access to communication of their wants and needs.
- The Internet can provide access to communication for people who were previously cut off from such interaction.
- This communication can use older technologies such as fax as well as newer ones such as e-mail and on-line chat.
- Successful curricular e-mail projects need careful planning and firm timelines.
- Online chat will not be appropriate in many educational environments but, properly managed, it may have a role with older students.
- The availability of cheaper digital cameras means that communication which has previously been textual will involve images in future.

References

Abbott, C. (2000) *ICT: Changing Education*, London: RoutledgeFalmer.

ASHA (1992) *A Communication Bill of Rights*, National Joint Committee for the Communication Needs of Persons with Severe Disabilities, Rockville MD: American Speech–Language–Hearing Association.

Banes, D., and Walter, R. (2000) *Internet for All*, London: David Fulton.

Dery, M. (ed.) (1994) *Flame Wars: The Discourse of Cyberculture*, Durham NC: Duke University Press.

Jones, S. G. (ed.) (1997) *Virtual Culture: Identity and Communication in Cybersociety*, London: Sage.

Nicholls, D. (1997) *Pooling Ideas on Art and Imaging*, Stoke-on-Trent: Trentham Books.

Strate, L., Jacobson, R., and Gibson, S. (eds) (1996) *Communication and Cyberspace: Social Interaction in an Electronic Environment*, Cresskill NJ: Hampton Press.

Turkle, S. (1984) *Second Self: Computers and the Human Spirit*, New York: Simon and Schuster.

Turkle, S. (1996) *Life on the Screen: Identity in the Age of the Internet*, London: Weidenfeld and Nicolson.

Chapter 7

Spike the bear and an on-line special school

David Ware

In his description of the development of whole-school ICT resources at a school for children with learning difficulties, ICT co-ordinator David Ware explains how a range of projects have helped children learn more effectively and develop a growing sense of their place in the world.

At Little Heath School we have been exploring the relationship between information and communications technology (ICT) and the achievement of young people with a variety of learning difficulties (special educational needs, SEN). It is still relatively early days, but it is clear from the work undertaken so far that developments involving multi-media, networking and computer communications represent previously unimagined opportunities to motivate and encourage young people with special educational needs. These technologies can also raise their self-esteem and overcome their feelings of failure, inadequacy and isolation.

For many young people with special educational needs, these aspects are of critical importance. In our experience, young people with learning difficulties really do want to learn but their difficulties pose significant barriers to this and result in academic and personal failure and feelings of anger, frustration and disillusionment with the education system. The effects can all too readily be seen in quiet withdrawal from the process of lessons, underachievement, periods of disaffection, reluctance to engage appropriately with the learning process, emotional outbursts, incidents of inappropriate behaviour and the like.

The link between ICT and achievement: one school's story

Little Heath School is a special school for 150 such young people in north-east London. Aged between 11 and 19 years, they have a wide range of special educational needs, including speech, language and communication difficulties, epilepsy, autism, cerebral palsy, general and specific learning difficulties, dyspraxia, Asperger's syndrome, attention deficit and hyperactivity disorders and emotional and behavioural problems. Supporting young people with these kinds of difficulties requires sensitivity to their learning and development needs and a clear and supportive structure in which those needs can be met. For teachers, the facilities provided by an increasingly wide range of computer software programs and hardware devices offer a comprehensive set of additional tools to help in meeting these requirements. They also offer opportunities for sharing information, developing new and exciting ways of working and reducing the bureaucratic work load associated with the modern education system.

The development of ICT at the school is founded on the firm belief that, for young people with learning difficulties, ICT provides significant opportunities for helping them to be independent and responsible learners and to develop essential skills for their present and future lives. What we do about providing these opportunities depends on our enthusiasm, creativity and commitment. We can encourage these through establishing an ambitious vision about how ICT can help in raising pupil achievement, actively involving the whole school population in key areas of development, and developing a high profile for ICT by publicising successes and achievements and keeping everyone informed. We also need access to high-quality resources, dependable levels of support and adequate time for enquiry and reflection.

Since 1997 the school has made a significant investment in developing a computer network, with more than seventy stations, serving the whole school. There are at least three computers in every classroom, including the library, and two well equipped ICT resource rooms. All the computers are connected to two central network servers. The key factor that enabled this to happen was the ability to persuade the head teacher and senior managers of the benefits for the school of developing ICT. This, along with good planning processes, enabled us to employ support, particularly technical help, where and when it was needed. It also helped us to provide facilities and access to resources which were useful for teachers in supporting learning.

At Little Heath School the computer network encourages, promotes and supports the use of ICT in all curriculum areas. Its development reflects and reinforces whole-school policies particularly those in relation to the curriculum, teaching and learning and equal opportunities. It achieves this through providing a consistent look; a common procedure for using computers across the school; central storage facilities; the ability to develop work on different computers at different times; protection of essential system and users' work files; daily backup of network data; facilities for managing user work, sharing files and information and communicating between computers. Whilst there are difficulties associated with the management of computer networks for busy teachers, the advantages of network technologies far outweigh the disadvantages. In our experience, each of these aspects and the employment of a member of staff with expertise in computer networking are essential to ensuring that the development of ICT across the whole school is successful.

The school has developed a wide range of facilities to ensure that pupils can access the technology and the growing range of opportunities provided by the Internet and World Wide Web. We use commercial software such as the Microsoft Office suite of programs, but complement their use with a range of specialist and supporting tools. These include speech feedback and text-reading software, templates, and models and frameworks which can be modified and adapted for individual use. We also use a range of SEN-specific programs (such as My World, Clicker and Inclusive Writer) and multimedia resources in the form of images (clip art and photographs), sounds and, increasingly, video. All pupils study for nationally recognised examinations in ICT in Years 10 and 11 and all leavers are presented with a CD-ROM containing all their work done on the computer network whilst at the school to enable progression to further education.

Developing a school intranet

The school intranet is a focal point of the school's work with computers. It is a showcase for pupils' work, a mirror on the life of the school and a growing resource for subjects of the curriculum, with appropriate Internet links and learning resources developed by both pupils and staff. The intranet uses sound in the form of voice-recorded files and images to ease navigation, and solves some of the problems associated with Internet access such as limited bandwidth and the often inaccessible nature of the information and resources available through the Internet for young people with special educational needs.

The Geography Web, for example, contains images of the local area for use by pupils in urban and rural studies, links with Web sites found by pupils and staff and learning materials downloaded from the Internet and modified for pupil use. Other subject Webs contain staff-developed quizzes and on-line worksheets and reference materials. We are particularly indebted to the work of Barbara Garrison, English teacher and Netlinks co-ordinator at Mar Vista Middle School in San Diego, California, for her help in this aspect of our work. Without her creativity, inspiration and enthusiasm some of the work described in this case study would simply not have been possible.

Easing access to Internet resources is the main aim of Barbara's Netlinks Project. A Netlink is a lesson or project which comprises tasks and activities with links for learners to appropriate Internet sites. It is rather like the traditional worksheet which lists the resources available to complete tasks, but in this case the worksheet is an HTML text with embedded hyperlinks to relevant Web sites for resources and reference material. A Netlink avoids the difficulties associated with inexperienced learners finding appropriate sites to complete tasks. The lesson or project can also be differentiated according to the needs of learners, and as such is a safe and reliable approach to utilising the range of resources available through the Internet. These facilities can also help to ameliorate some of the difficulties associated with what an education consultant colleague has called 'one-chance learning' (Davitt 2000). Pupils returning to school after a period of absence can be directed to the on-line learning resources to help fill in some of the gaps they may have experienced in their learning as a result of their absence.

Pupils can also use the intranet to develop and publish their own Web sites and learning resources. In this way they gain an appreciation and understanding of the nature and structure of the World Wide Web as well as contributing something of value to the learning of others.

Tinu (Year 9) writes poetry and publishes selected examples on the school intranet; Jane (Year 10) has developed a useful resource about how to look after guineapigs; and Sunita (17 years old) has created an interactive Powerpoint presentation of images and sounds to assist younger pupils in learning the alphabet. Turning pupil work produced on the computer into material which can be accessed by others through the technology of the Internet adds a purposeful dimension to work done at school that is yet to be fully exploited, but represents a potential for raising student achievement that is the stuff of professional dreams.

This could not be better reinforced than through experiencing the emotions of a 16-year-old girl with a history of academic failure seeing her interactive multimedia presentation being used by other pupils to learn about the life and work of Vincent Van Gogh, or seeing the pride felt by Year 8 pupils and teachers when an e-mail message from a 20-year-old African student was received. He had responded to their online presentation about illness and disease by saying how valuable he found the work in informing his own research.

A feature of the intranet and the school's Web site is that both feature collections of photographs taken by pupils and staff using digital cameras, to record the weekly life of the school. They are accessible to everyone and provide concrete recognition of participation in school life as well as celebrating pupil and staff successes. They are used as resources for a wide variety of school purposes, including school brochures, newsletters and publicity material. Pupils, in particular, respond positively to the wealth of image resources available, and use them to reflect school life and support written tasks, and as representations of achievement. For young people who experience difficulties with the written word these images provide an alternative means of communicating that comes directly from their own experience and which encourages success and reduces the incidence of failure.

The school intranet includes a separate teacher web which recognises the different purposes to which the technology can be put for this group. Whilst the pupil webs are accessible to all users of the network, the teacher web is password-protected. It provides facilities for communicating and sharing ideas, access to on-line resources and training materials and opportunities for publicising school developments and priorities. One member of staff has developed a web of useful images, sound and video resources which pupils and other staff can use in the development of their own Web sites and for work with a variety of software programmes. Other staff have created models and ideas which represent ways in which pupils can use the technology to communicate and present work in ways which are exciting and avoid some of the pitfalls associated with traditional methods of communicating and presenting work in schools.

All pupils at the school have their own e-mail address, but often lack the skills and understanding to make effective use of it. As a result, the school has developed e-mail projects with a number of schools around the world. These projects are subject to careful and detailed plans, developed in co-operation with partner schools, and provide mutually beneficial outcomes for participants. One school has even used pupils at Little Heath to help with the acquisition of the English language. For young people with language and communication difficulties, this is a significant achievement that has resulted in improvements in pupil motivation, independence and responsibility, and an increase in the appropriate use of e-mail amongst the pupil population.

The SpikeNet story

SpikeNet is an exciting development that has arisen out of the e-mail work of the school. Spike, a teddy bear named by pupils at the school, accompanies pupils on school visits, travels to schools in other countries and keeps a record of his visits through photographs and diary entries. Younger (and older!) pupils can keep in touch with him through his Web site and e-mail and, in this way, are encouraged to develop their learning and communication skills and find out about people and places in other parts of the world.

To date, Spike has visited the United States, Turkey, Spain, France and Austria: arrangements are in hand to extend his travels. Through this project, pupils can become virtual visitors to other countries and gain some experience of what life may be like in places that they may never visit. These virtual visits have generated an enthusiasm for electronic communication amongst pupils and provided concrete support for broadening pupils' horizons and for the improvement of their social skills and understanding of other societies, peoples and cultures, a key aim of the school in its work with young people. The use of a travelling teddy bear has also resulted in positive responses from the broader community, including business organisations.

Another exciting development is a networked radio station, Little Heath Radio, which makes good use of the sound facilities of modern computers. The radio station provides opportunities for pupils to practise and develop their communication skills by acting as disc jockeys, news readers and weather forecasters. It has still further potential that has yet to be explored, but the radio station provides opportunities to bring together the whole school community in ways that are relevant and meaningful, and reflect life outside school. The ICT department has taken part in video-conferencing between pupils and teachers attending training sessions elsewhere in the country. Prearranged net meetings were set up with groups of teachers on in-service training days led by ICT and English consultant John Davitt. Pupils had previously examined an ancient giant cockleshell and had written down questions to ask the owner, John, about it. As the questions are asked it turns out that the shell was found buried in a garden near an old Roman road, well away from the sea and accompanied by traces of a fire. A historical mystery then unfolds between two remote audiences, providing a stimulating context for questioning and response to questions.

This use of video-conferencing with clear purposes, pre-planned activities and preparatory classwork allowed pupils to practise and develop their language and communication skills and provided teachers with living proof of the benefits of ICT for pupils with special educational needs.

> When we had finished our live video conference, there was a hushed silence in the room – here was a technology finally meeting a real need – providing equality of access and giving a voice to those often denied such opportunities in the past.
>
> (Davitt 2000)

This story of Little Heath School and its work with ICT is an on-going one. We have come a long way in just four years and pupils are responding to developments with improvements in levels of literacy, learning and communication skills, self-confidence and self-esteem, increased willingness to engage in the learning process and enthusiasm for the range of facilities provided by the technology. Plans are in hand to build on these successes through additional investments in multimedia technologies, making significant changes to the environment within which the technology is located, and increasing access to the technology by opening our facilities beyond normal school hours. We also hope to arrange student loans of computers, develop on-line communities and provide opportunities for pupils to act as advocates of ICT through taking responsibility for developments both within the school and beyond.

We are only just beginning to fully understand the potential of the technology for improving the learning experience of young people with learning difficulties. There is a degree of risk taking involved and a significant amount of work, but we are convinced from the evidence we have gathered so far that there really is no limit to what young people with learning difficulties can do with ICT. Once schools and teachers provide the opportunities that our young people need, the only limit to what is possible is that set by our own imaginations.

Summary

- A clear vision is needed about what ICT can do for the school.
- Firm belief in the value of ICT to the work of the school needs to underpin the curriculum.

- A well planned development programme for ICT encourages a shared commitment to improvement and expansion.
- Schools need an enthusiastic ICT co-ordinator who understands clearly how ICT can help develop learning and communication skills in pupils.
- Good technician support for developing ICT allows problems to be solved and new initiatives to take place.
- Good teacher knowledge of using ICT systems maximises their potential for supporting learning.
- A proactive approach should be taken when presenting the achievements of pupils to a wider audience.
- Teachers should develop an attitude that does not accept limitations as to what pupils with SEN can do when using ICT.

Reference

Davitt, J. (2000) Press release, available on-line at www.littleheath.essex.sch.uk/ press.htm (accessed 20 June 2001).

Chapter 8

Literacy and communication through ICT and the Internet for deaf children

Ken Carter, Matthew James and Helen Lansdown

Learning from their work at the Deafax Trust, the authors of this chapter explore the ways in which new technologies can have particular benefits for young people who are deaf or whose hearing is impaired. They also indicate the need for research into the precise nature of the support that ICT and the Internet can offer this target group.

ICT has changed my life and that of my family and opened up new possibilities and opportunities for other deaf people like myself. Through the Internet I have the world at my fingertips.

(Chair of Deafax 2001)

Partly in response to profound statements coming from deaf children and adults about the power of ICT and the Internet, the Deafax Trust has been embracing the global aspects of this communications network for nearly two decades. The word Internet is an abbreviation of 'international' and 'network' and is most easily described as millions of computers linked up so that they talk to one another. If you can read and write, you can use the Internet to look for answers to every question posed, send messages and documents anywhere, shop for things you want or look for books to read. You may also play games, chat, read the news in any language, learn sign languages, link with deaf and hearing people with similar interests, search for free software or while away your time surfing the net and exploring new areas of possible interest. In some respects the Internet is not just about computers, it is about people communicating and sharing knowledge.

Establishing Deafax

Whilst the Internet was conceived around forty years ago for mainly military purposes which then led on to research and academic use, it was later taken up by the financial sector. This in turn led to its final and arguably most important phase in becoming a network for all. In 1985 the Deafax Trust was set up by deaf and hearing people to both exploit and participate in this ICT revolution, but for the benefit of deaf children. Its mission has been, since its inception, to lead by example and identify, and promote and implement solutions that enable deaf children to communicate confidently and effectively with everyone. Literacy is a more complex concept than merely the practicalities inherent in the process of reading and writing: it is inextricably rooted in interaction with others. Unfortunately, deaf children are all too often assessed and judged on what they are unable to do. It may well be more meaningful to address the need for a closer relationship between theory, assessment, curriculum and practice in their overall education.

Deafax has sought to ensure, through its pioneering work, that deaf adults are more equipped to compete with others and secure decision-making positions. They provide added value by acting as role models to a growing generation of deaf children. At every opportunity it has promoted and practised a deaf and hearing partnership approach. Since 1985 a range of innovative projects have been introduced to, and implemented with, a wide range of deaf children, their parents or guardians and teachers.

One of the formative projects was Telephones for Deaf Children, which was focused in and around Berkshire and involved fourteen textphones for the equivalent number of children and their families together with four deaf adults. The aim was to train them in the use of the textphone and provide them with opportunities to use it interactively with others and to then measure any improvement in their communication and literacy levels. The deaf adults would telephone the deaf children at agreed times during the week to discuss a variety of topics. The children were also encouraged to link up with one another.

The outcomes were very positive. The children were highly motivated to keep in contact with one another, and they compiled records of each call, becoming increasingly independent in initiating and receiving calls and relying less on their parents. It was agreed by the parents that there was an improvement in their communications skills and their use of English during conversations. In the second year of the project British Telecom (BT) became involved. This was a significant

The 'I Can' statements	Unit four Communicating in writing
Level one	I can: • Tell you what a letter is for. • Write a letter. • Put an address on an envelope. • Send a letter. • Tell you two different costs for sending a letter. • Tell you how long letters should take to arrive.
Level two	I can: • Tell you what a fax machine does. • Send a fax. • Receive a fax. • Tell you when the paper is running out and put more paper in.
Level three	I can: • Set the fax to receive on auto or manual. • Use the fax with the speakerphone/monitor key or the handset. • Programme the date and time and name and fax number.

Figure 8.1 The 'I can' statements for communicating in writing

development, especially as the company was seen as a world leader in telecommunications.

From this programme evolved the Deafax TCL (Telecommunications and Literacy) for Children project, sponsored by the BBC Children in Need appeal fund for over nine years, and which has led to the Deafchild UK ICT Training Programme. 'I can' statements are used as part of a pragmatic approach to training deaf children to understand more fully the concepts behind communication. Assistance from a selected number of teachers of the deaf has ensured that it can be used to support parts of the National Curriculum.

The Deafchild ICT Training Programme has four units and three levels. Unit one is concerned with 'Learning about Communication' unit two with 'Communicating by Telephone' unit three with 'Communicating by Textphone' and unit four with 'Communicating by Writing' (using letters and fax machines).

Level one is a relatively straightforward introduction to each unit. The statements each serve to highlight the area of competence eventually expected of the pupils. They should, following training, be able to say 'I can' and for their level of competence to be measurable. The starting point for all the units will depend upon the age and experience of the pupils. The concept of letter writing has been included because it is a basic form of distance communication still widely used and not requiring equipment. It also serves as a good basis for the work using fax machines and then e-mail and discussion around the ways of speeding up the communication by the writing process. Throughout, the pupils are given opportunities of hands-on experience.

Level two, unit four, encourages the children to think further about the use of writing. They will have established that one way of communicating is by writing a letter but that this can take at least one day and often longer. The concept of the fax machine is then introduced: a quicker way of sending writing and pictures. Following a simple explanation the pupils have an opportunity to use the fax machine and to receive and send both manually and automatically.

In level three children are shown that programming the date, time, name and fax number on the fax machine is not difficult. It is necessary, however, to ensure that the pupils understand and can explain the reasons why it is useful to have this information printed out automatically on the fax messages they send and receive, for example because it helps to identify the sender.

Moving forward: the Internet

In response to the success of this programme and a full evaluation of the resources and training involved, it was decided that a further training manual should be produced which would focus in more depth on the role that computers and video-conferencing can play in supporting deaf children as they develop their skills in, and awareness of, ICT. It was entitled the ICT for Children Programme. The Internet offers a rich source of information with which to augment daily teaching and learning activities. The main beneficiary of this global network is not the business community, nor is it the average user at home; the people with the most to gain from the Internet are teachers and their pupils. To this end a highly visual training manual (using graphics and pictures) covering the basics of computing, the Internet and video-conferencing was devised.

The programme is modular and is designed to be applicable to deaf children across the Key Stages. Communicating by e-mail really does lend itself to use by deaf children, because it is typical that this form of correspondence is kept short, and concise paragraphs are preferable to longwinded ones. Not everyone using e-mail speaks English as a first language and users of this mode of communication tend to be more accepting of any mistakes made.

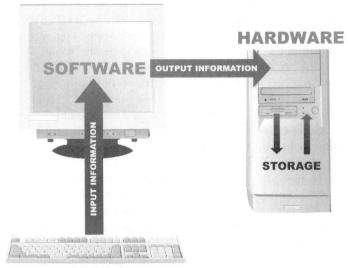

Figure 8.2 A computer input and output

Typical WWW address:

http://www.bbc.co.uk

Hyper Text Transfer Protocol   World Wide Web   Name of Company
(language between computer)

Hyper means fast   Type of business
Text is the language form
Terminal computer   From the United Kingdom
Protocol is the proper way to do things

Search

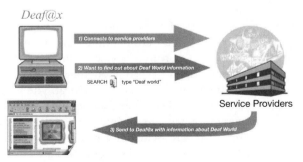

Figure 8.3 What is the Internet?

The Deafax ICT Programme has seven modules which cover 'Computers and how they work', 'Surfing the World Wide Web', 'Sending and receiving e-mails', 'Video-conferencing – seeing you, seeing me', 'Creating with Powerpoint', 'Working with spreadsheets' and 'Working with a database'. As the children progress through these modules they are introduced to a highly visual way of understanding the concepts and language used.

Each module has been assessed by a qualified teacher of the deaf. This ensures that it is suitable to be used with a particular age range and classroom application, so that it can be used by teachers following training and support from Deafax.

As a result of developing the above programme, Deafax embarked upon another scheme known as Fax Buddies. This initiative was a collaborative partnership between BT, the National Council for Educational Technology (NCET, now known as BECTA) and Deafax. The aim was to evaluate the uses and benefits of the fax machine for deaf children.

At eight schools 150 children were linked with adult employees of BT, NCET and the DfEE. Over a period of twelve weeks 950 faxes from every child and fax buddy were collated for analysis and used in an evaluation report. From the findings there was considerable evidence of greater awareness in the sequencing of messages and writing for a purpose; better drafting and redrafting leading to improved spelling and punctuation; and the development of a greater range of language use such as replying to questions, passing on news and making statements.

Whilst developing the many schemes concerned with ICT, literacy and communication, Deafax has been extremely mindful of the National Curriculum Key Stages, especially relating to English (reading and writing). Figures 8.4–8 were devised to highlight particular areas which deaf children, in general, find challenging. It also emphasises how ICT and the Internet can be exploited to help and encourage deaf children to reach the attainment targets.

The New Opportunities Fund (NOF) for ICT training of teachers, which was set up by the UK government through the Teacher Training Agency, gave Deafax the opportunity to take the initiative. It was decided to set up a consortium to apply to become an Approved Training Provider specialising in the training of teachers of the deaf. The programme is known as Deafchild UK ICT Teacher Training. The modules on offer consist of communication techniques, Internet use, the preparation and delivery of teaching materials, useful software, and literacy and numeracy strategies using ICT. The teachers who are trained are not expected to become ICT specialists, but they are enabled to become effective teachers who are competent with ICT.

Attainment target	Pupils learn to speak clearly, thinking about the needs of their listeners. They work in small groups and as a class, joining in discussions and making relevant points. They learn to use language in imaginative ways and express their ideas and feelings when working in role and drama activities.
Problems encountered by deaf children	Some concepts can be abstract to children until they have 'hands on' experience. Children do not always expect to take responsibility for – or consider the implications of – using equipment. They should be encouraged to assess and discuss the appropriateness of different equipment for use in a range of situations and to become independent users.
How ICT supports attainment	The Internet, faxing and using textphones provide a basis from which learning and developing communication skills can be acquired. Faxing and using the textphone in varying situations and to a wide range of people can reinforce the concept of register and appropriate responses.

Figure 8.4 National Curriculum English Key Stage 1 and deaf children:
(1) Speaking and listening

Attainment target	Pupils' interest and pleasure in reading are developed as they learn to read confidently and independently. They focus on words and sentences and how they fit into whole texts.
Problems encountered by deaf children	As deaf children often struggle with reading, they may lack incentive and regard reading as a chore rather than as fun and a way to explore the imagination. They may not understand the purpose of reading and feel despondent, especially if they see their hearing peers beginning to read more effectively. This begins to affect their confidence and demotivates them.
How ICT supports attainment	By communicating on a regular basis via technology (fax and e-mail buddies) the children are given a tangible incentive to read. They begin to spot familiar words in context, and use these words in their own writing, to reinforce meaning and register. Reading is no longer regarded as a chore, nor is it limited to books; the children begin to realise that reading has a purpose in everyday life. This opens up a whole new world of communication at a distance.

Figure 8.5 National Curriculum English Key Stage 1 and deaf children:
(2) Reading

Attainment target	Pupils should be taught to use a range of strategies to make sense of what they read, this includes:

- *Phonic knowledge*: recognise, consider and identify alliteration, syllables, initial and final sounds in words, inconsistencies in phonic patterns.
- *Graphic knowledge*: plurals, spelling patterns in verb endings, relations between root words and derivatives, prefixes and suffixes, inflectional endings.
- *Word recognition*: recognise words with common spelling patterns.
- *Grammatical awareness*: recognise the value of surrounding text in identifying unknown words, work out the sense of the text by reading ahead.
- *Contextual understanding*: focus on text meaning as a whole.

Problems encountered by deaf children	Where the first language is British Sign Language (BSL), children tend to write English using BSL grammatical structure. It is clear how their first language, which has no written form, influences the development of their English literacy. Many deaf children, not just those whose first language is BSL, find difficulty in using tense, conjunctions, prepositions and many other features of English grammar. The reason for this is, in part, because many features of English are not present in BSL. As deaf children do not hear spoken English, the reinforcement is not present and acquisition is delayed. Greater visual stimulus is required to reinforce English grammatical features.
How ICT supports attainment	Software packages (e.g. Deafax, *Around the House*) can incorporate visual stimuli plus sign language (BSL/SSE) to reinforce grammar. Comparisons between BSL and English can be made by exploiting technology e.g. digital cameras, sign language CD-ROMs and subtitled videos. Also, by communicating regularly, children will begin to gather experience of context (register, relevant responses to topics, etc.) and word patterns. Regular communication should lead to increased word recognition as the children begin to use new words in their responses.

Figure 8.6 National Curriculum English Key Stage I and deaf children: (3) Reading

Attainment target	Pupils should understand the value of writing as a means of communicating meaning in narrative and non-fiction texts, and to spell and punctuate properly.
Problems encountered by deaf children	Deaf children can find writing a chore and some even have a 'fear of writing', often as a result of feeling their writing is inferior to that of their hearing peers. This leads to demotivation and the belief that they may never write adequately or well.
How ICT supports attainment	Often children learn best when having fun. Technology (Internet, computers, games and other visual ICT) can create an enjoyable and imaginative learning experience. When technology is used for communicating, deaf children begin to see a purpose to writing (Writing KS1), especially when they receive a response, or make a new friend (Fax Buddies and e-mailing Penpals via the Deafchild International Fun Club). Isolated deaf children are encouraged to 'belong' and have the incentive to use and improve their literacy levels, knowing their writing has a readership.

Figure 8.7 National Curriculum English Key Stage 1 and deaf children: (4) Writing

Attainment target	Pupils should be taught to consider the composition of their writing and to work with others to plan and draft in order to develop their writing. Punctuation helps a reader understand what has been written and develop effective strategies for spelling and checking spelling.
Problems encountered by deaf children	Many deaf children encounter particular problems with punctuation and spelling.
How ICT supports attainment	With technology becoming more accessible, children – potentially – enjoy greater exposure to written text than at any time in the past. This has a profound impact on their writing. By becoming active participants in a communication process which involves technology (faxing, textphone, dialogues, etc.) they will also be exposed more often to a wider vocabulary and more sophisticated grammatical structures. ICT can be used to target literacy development.

Figure 8.8 National Curriculum English Key Stage 1 and deaf children: (5) Writing

Deafchild International

Deafax, as part of its strategy, has always promoted better communication and literacy for deaf children worldwide. By winning a Cable and Wireless Childnet International Web site competition it had the opportunity to create and develop a unique Web site, Deafchild International (www. deafchild.org). The Deafchild International Web site features the following zones: an international directory of deaf schools, an international directory of video-conferencing contacts, staff exchanges and visits for key trainers, competitions, teachers' forum, parents' forum, Technology Advisory Forum and a showcase of deaf role models. The statistics relating to the site at the end of March 2001 were: 617 registered partners in thirty countries; 145 registered schools in twenty-three countries; over 250,000 hits on the Web site during a twelve-month period alone, twenty role models interviewed, profiled and linked with deaf children, 52 per cent under 18 years old; and 69 per cent deaf users. The Deafchild team has visited schools for the deaf in Australia, New Zealand, Barbados, the United States, the Czech Republic, India and the Republic of Ireland, where deaf children face challenges in literacy development, and have promoted the work of Deafchild International.

ICT Research Unit

As Deafax has operated as a catalyst for change since 1985 it was seen to be important to conduct research into the benefits or otherwise of our work. This was done in partnership with the Research Group for Inclusive Environments at the University of Reading. The DfEE sponsored Phase 1 of ICT, Achievement and the Education of Deaf Children. The information and data which have been collated and analysed in the different sections have acted as an important baseline to use over the next three phases of the programme. The main outcomes of this first-ever study were as follows:

• The Deafax Trust, through using deaf and hearing people as role models, has been responsible through its ICT programmes from 1988 to 2001 for ensuring that many deaf children, their parents and teachers have been introduced to ICT for educational and social purposes. It has acted as a catalyst of change by using ICT to improve literacy and communication skills. There is considerable evidence to show that its innovative work has made a significant ·difference to the quality of life of many deaf children. Ongoing evaluations of its programmes are being documented.

- The Deafchild UK Millennium Conference 'Improving Literacy Skills of Deaf Children through ICT' concluded that teachers, parents, deaf adults and others need to embrace ICT as an educational tool to ensure that an interactive environment is created both at home and at school.

- Whilst the ICT literature review revealed some significant studies in the areas of word-processing, electronic communication, computers as a teaching resource, multimedia authoring, videoconferencing and speech recognition concerning deaf children, there was no research into the relationship between ICT and standards in deaf education. Other phases of this research programme will need to work with BECTA and OFSTED to ascertain ways of measuring deaf pupils' attainments and the use of ICT.

- The national surveys from 191 institutions and representing the ICT environments of 3,000 deaf pupils revealed some interesting information about staff, communication, ICT background, ICT facilities, use of packages and achievements. It could be stated that whilst there seems to be a range of ICT equipment available, there are problems using it. The majority of deaf pupils, according to the information given by the teachers, do not use ICT equipment at home; the amount of use of ICT resources by teachers and pupils would suggest that it plays a minor role at this point in time; and the levels of ICT skills and knowledge are difficult to gauge. However, the indicators would suggest that advice, support and specific training are required by the majority.

- The case studies verified many of the findings listed from the surveys. There was a realisation on the part of all the teachers that ICT was going to play a greater role in the on-going future education of deaf children and that they need to have far more training to improve their skills and knowledge. Technology was only as good as the teachers using it.

- The environments in which ICT was used were generally good but there were clear conflicts in providing a lighting regime which meets the needs of both the pupils and the teachers.

- The Deafchild UK ICT Teacher Training (NOF/TTA) programme is fulfilling an urgent need to provide specialist training for teachers of the deaf in ICT skills to benefit themselves and their pupils. As the teacher training programme is not yet over, it was deemed inappropriate to analyse the individualised needs assessment carried out with teachers participating in the training. This will be included in subsequent phases of the research programme.

- ICT has, through this programme, been identified as one of the most significant influences in the future development of deaf education.

One of the conclusions at the Deafchild UK Millennium Conference, to which the Minister for Learning and Technology contributed, was that reading and writing skills would become increasingly important in the twenty-first century. The Internet is revolutionising the way we communicate with one another. Families will need more support with ICT so that their children will benefit and not be left out. Social inclusion needs to be high on our agenda when we consider deaf children's education both in the home and at school. Learning is a social and communication process.

The ever mounting pressure from the government to increase ICT provision in schools has been highlighted by a series of government initiatives which have been welcomed by teachers, parents, academics, deaf adults and organisations concerned with the education of deaf children.

The rate of developments in ICT and the Internet and their relevance to the education of deaf children is increasing. However, the long-term benefits will follow only when the results of this on-going research inform, develop and manage the education of deaf children and those who communicate with them.

ICT and the Internet are being recognised differently throughout the world and in those countries that invest in its development within education. It is vital that such developments are shared and disseminated and that cross-fertilisation of ideas can take place. Deafax will continue to seek a major role in this process as a catalyst of change.

Summary

- The use of fax by deaf children has been highly successful and has paved the way for Internet use.
- Structured programmes such as that developed by Deafax help deaf children make best use of technology.
- Training for teachers is essential.
- Research is needed into the links between ICT and achievement in deaf education.

References

Carter, K.C., Wald, M., Lansley, P.R. and Bright, K. (2001) *Deafax/IE: ICT, Achievement and the Education of Deaf Children, DfEE Research Report, Phase 1, 2001*, London: DfEE.

Deafax (1995) *BBC Children in Need Report: The First Phase. Telecommunications for Deaf Children, 1992–95*, Reading: Deafax.

Deafax (1997a) *TCL for Children Programme, Levels 1, 2, 3*, Reading: Deafax.

Deafax (1997b) *Cheerful Charlie visits Deafax House. Deafax Literacy Project, Unit 1 'Around the House'*, Reading: Deafax.

Deafax (1998) *BBC Children in Need Report: The Second Phase. Deafchild UK – Telecommunications and Information Network for Deaf Children, 1995–98*, Reading: Deafax.

Deafax (1999) *Deafchild UK ICT for Children Programme, 1999*, Reading: Deafax.

Deafax (1999) *Introduction to the Internet, World Wide Web (WWW) and Electronic Mail (e-mail)*, Reading: Deafax.

Deafax (2001) *Deafchild UK TCLC (Telecommunications and Literacy for Children Programme), Levels 1, 2, 3, 1997–2001*, Reading: Deafax.

James, M. (2000) 'The Deafchild International Web Site and Learning Technologies as Education and Learning Tools to develop Deaf Children's Literacy and Communication Skills', paper presented at the nineteenth International Congress on Education of the Deaf, 9–13 July.

Chapter 9

Swanseekers
Using stories to develop on-line environmental education

Maggie Pollard

> Describing her experience as the head teacher of a special school in Glasgow, Maggie Pollard shares some of the key principles which she and her staff have found to be vital for successful use of the Internet to develop environmental awareness and promote inclusion.

We began our journey with technology when Richmond Park School, a special school in Glasgow for primary-age children who have a significant physical disability, first connected with computers in the mid-1980s. Children who for years had struggled to find a voice, both literally and metaphorically, started to communicate using basic cause-and-effect software, simple graphic programs, word processing and even electronic mail. Teachers too found a voice. And, as they witnessed, for example, those pupils who could not grasp a pencil to form letters beginning to write using a keyboard, they began to wonder what else could be achieved with the help of computers.

Teachers at Richmond Park have now stopped asking what this technology is capable of, since we have seen a wide range of possibilities. The emphasis now is on using the technology to support the teaching and learning process. This may seem like a simple change in semantics but it masks a profound change in thinking for this school in inner-city Glasgow.

Beginnings

Our journey with technology has sometimes been exciting, innovative, challenging and relentless. It has, however, always been fun. That has been the case from the time when the first government initiative saw the delivery of a big brown box housing a single BBC computer to our school to, in this new millennium, New Opportunities Fund (NOF) funding for whole-school networking and staff training. Our growing understanding of the potential of the technology has assuredly given us a voice as we have enthusiastically and determinedly shared the knowledge that we have gained about the positive impact of ICT on pupil and teacher learning.

For many schools which are nearer the beginning of their journey or which are struggling down the road burdened with curricular and social pressures, it may not seem like fun. ICT and the Internet might not be seen as a solution to problems of attainment and achievement, and they may even be seen as something else that just has to be fitted into an overcrowded school day. However, if you read one of the stories on our Web site (www.btinternet.com/~richmond.park) and read it in the knowledge that, like all schools, we are expected to meet a wide range of learners' needs within a framework of government policies, then you too may be happy to continue with this great ICT challenge.

Inclusion and special schools

Like many other special schools, we have to cater for physical, medical, specific, moderate to severe learning difficulties, behavioural and emotional problems. Our school is adjacent to one of Glasgow's many parks, Richmond Park. This park, with its boating pond, is also home to many swans and, logically, swans have been adopted for the school logo. When planning an environmental studies programme for the four senior classes, teachers created the contexts for learning around the theme of swans and a story about them, *Swanseekers*. This story follows the flight of five swans, four of them in the direction of the four compass points to give a bird's-eye square-mile view of the local area, and one to open up the wider possibilities offered by the Internet.

The story tells how the swans love the children who go to this special school in the Gorbals district of Glasgow, and how they sometimes wonder why the children have to travel so many miles by taxi or bus to get to school. Raising this topic enables teachers to discuss issues such as social inclusion at a time when mainstreaming is a key issue for the new Scottish Executive.

We remember the arguments about integration when the Warnock report was published, and we feel strongly about access for children with disability. We are committed to equality of opportunity and equal rights and we fully support Sir William MacPherson's report (on the Stephen Lawrence inquiry) which states how important it is for communities to grow together and look after each other. But we are also pragmatic, and, in our understanding of discrimination and difference, we know that the ninety children in our school need a lot of support. Most of them require regular daily nursing or therapeutic intervention to help with their physical or medical difficulties. The teacher–pupil ratio in the school allows individualised educational plans (IEPs) to be drawn up by experienced and trained staff. There are many different agencies represented in the school, and all the people involved are learners too: teachers, nursery nurses, auxiliaries, nurses, speech and language therapists, occupational therapists, physiotherapists and pupils.

A shared vision, staff development and progression

In order for all these agencies to work together, it is vital that key principles are accepted by everyone; and many of these principles arose from work with technology. The first principle is about having a shared vision, which helps create an ethos of achievement for all. The second principle is about creative models of staff development. A cohort of postgraduate students from Strathclyde University and their lecturer came to the school to see how ICT was integrated into the teaching and learning process, and the staff of the school demonstrated this by putting on a show called 'A Touch of Magic'.

The in-service training session took place in the evening when all the children had gone home, and it was extremely successful. As an interactive model of staff development for both the staff and the students it had those ingredients about teaching and learning that the staff consider important, including their mantra: 'Be happy, be a learner'. The staff at the school really believe that learning should be fun, and they ask fundamental questions about how teachers teach and how learners learn. The staff have gained much empirical evidence about this over the years, and are now ready to share their understanding of topics such as knowledge and understanding, multiple and emotional intelligences and responding to different learning styles. They are also interested in how all that fits into their innovative work with ICT.

The third principle deals with the progression of skills. As head teacher I see this as the key expectation of our school and also the biggest challenge for teachers in special education. Many of the visitors who come to see ICT use in the school are interested most of all in this area. We hope that progression of skills is tangible, from the 5-year-olds in class 1, right through to the 12-year-olds in class 11, by which time you can see the development of word processing, graphics, audio and video into multimedia presentations.

Swanseekers

We aim to provide an environment where everyone can consider themselves a learner, whether they are 5 or 65. The *Swanseekers* story and e-mail project aims to illustrate this with an exciting, imaginative, cultural and aesthetic flight of a square-mile bird's-eye view of the school and its local environment. In the story, swan number one flies north with one class for a mile, swan number two flies south with its class, and swans number three and four fly east and west with their classes.

In the story, the swan that flies north visits museums and historic places such as Glasgow Green, the People's Palace, the cathedral and the oldest house in Glasgow. Children following this story learn some well known Glasgow street songs so that they can put on a recital at the People's Palace and learn about the performing arts and audience awareness. It does their self-esteem no end of good to have to perform, and of course there are so many ancillary activities involved, such as designing and making posters and programmes using our computers. I do hope the customers of the People's Palace tea room enjoy the children's performance.

The swan that flies south visits the Hampden Football Stadium, football being a popular topic for most of the pupils. The swan flying west encourages the pupils to use a variety of technology such as computers and digital video cameras to create a Gorbals tour for the school Web site. This multimedia program will use graphics, text, digital photography, film and audio to record the children's visit through the Gorbals.

An added bonus of this kind of multimedia authoring work is that the product is available to show when others such as HM inspectors may be charged with assessing what has been achieved in the school. Accountability has a particular significance for teachers working with special children, and with so much anecdotal evidence clouding the issues around ICT the school has to be rigorous in gathering hard evidence. It is also necessary to ensure that computers are integrated into our national curriculum guidelines.

The five Cs in action

At Richmond Park we have attempted to categorise what we believe to be essential life skills for children as the five Cs: collaboration, communication, critical thinking, creativity, computers. We aim to incorporate all these skills on our Gorbals tour as we study the history that leads us west. We have also done things a bit differently more recently. The teachers planned their programme with the children so that their interests could be taken on board too, and collaboratively they devised a topic called 'The Tram Ride'. Using a very technologically rich backdrop of digital video and special effects lighting, the sixteen children enacted a drama of what life was like in the early 1950s.

First they had to gather information about the past from local people, books, museums and the Internet, before scripting their imaginative story. They questioned what life must have been like, and by studying some artefacts such as ceramic hot water bottles, army helmets and chanties (chamber pots) they began to get a feel for the differences between the 1950s and today. They then began to write their story, which unfolds as an old Granny reflects on her youth when Frank Sinatra was an up-and-coming young crooner who wowed the girls. She remembers her life in the Gorbals as a girl when she and her friend Annie set off for a night in the nearby Princess Theatre to see, unfortunately, not Frank Sinatra but a local crooner called Kenneth McKellar. On the way to the theatre they pass children playing the old street games, of bools (marbles), skipping and peever (hopscotch). All this drama is acted out as the narrator links the unfolding story of the tram ride to the theatre.

It seems such a simple little drama, but the added dimension of integrating the really sophisticated technology of movies, interviews, titles, credits and video projector clearly shows the use of ICT as a powerful tool that supports teaching and learning. The story of 'The Tram Ride' can easily be exported to one of our school network partners. When we next video-conference with Bowmore Primary School, on the island of Islay, we can show them our video and discuss how they could become involved in our project. Even more interestingly, we could offer them our conceptual framework for the project, and they could make their own multimedia performance based on a ferry crossing of the 1950s.

Once again, the key to success in such a project is the consideration of the important factors, our five Cs:

- *Collaboration:* working together, networking, citizenship and sharing. This also involves respecting everyone's view and valuing each other, letting children take part in planning and designing their own curriculum.

- *Communication:* having the confidence to speak out, feeling good, having high self-esteem, knowing you'll be listened to. It's also about being able to communicate physically and intellectually; for that reason, some of the children use alternative communication aids or basic signing like Makaton. Computers have been a real asset to our communication, giving us opportunities for equality on the macro and micro scale.

- *Critical thinking:* how we use our brain to learn, which is a topic we address through what we call 'brain gym', or 'through mind mapping'. We also study accelerated learning programmes, and we think multiple and emotional intelligences play an important part in individual learning styles. If we want our children to be successful and fulfilled adults it is very important that they get sufficient help from us in learning how to learn.

- *Creativity:* the centre of all our activities, and also what our teachers demonstrate every day in the activities they plan. Given such a wide range of learners with their very individual needs, staff have to employ many different strategies, techniques and tools. Teachers always want the best for their pupils, and with access to all the new technologies the creative curriculum experience knows no bounds.

- *Computers.* With a school policy that states that the children we teach deserve the best resources, there is no restriction on computer equipment. There are many creative ways of funding these resources but there is no shortage of equipment and training. The most important thing to remember is that the new technologies are just tools. They are amazing tools and they enable us to do lots of creative work but, at the end of the day, it is what we do with them that is important. This is amply demonstrated by listening to what the teachers and pupils are saying and looking at what they are doing.

The role of the arts in an inclusive curriculum

The fourth swan leads the pupils towards an expressive arts-infused curriculum. Too often we leave the arts to the end, but we have a school belief in artists working with teachers and pupils to create resources such as an adventure east of the school in the grounds of Richmond Park itself. It was in this setting that the story of a little boy, aptly named Ritchie Park, was created. Ritchie's story is beautifully told in books that the children made themselves and then illustrated through puppetry and storytelling.

The teachers were delighted to have the Scottish Mask and Puppet Theatre working with them on this project and grateful to the Gorbals Social Inclusion Partnership and the Greater Glasgow Health Board for funding their involvement. It was good that the Scottish Arts Council then funded the TAG Theatre Company to work with the school on the further adventures of Ritchie Park. All these projects must subscribe to the principle that learning is fun and the 'Be happy, be a learner' slogan.

The Internet and global understanding

The fifth swan, a virtual swan perhaps, encourages pupils to think beyond the Gorbals by use of the Internet and the school's Web site. We have run e-mail and Internet projects with teachers, artists and policy makers, and using stories from Japan, America, South Africa, Australia, Estonia, Russia, Gran Canaria, Finland, Sweden and even Edinburgh. This has even managed to encourage some of the teachers to have global adventures themselves, and last year the physical education teacher and the computer teacher completed a multilingual magazine and video on Mobility and Movement that they produced in conjunction with colleagues from Finland and Gran Canaria. Their global adventures were funded through the EU Comenius Socrates programme, and cultural and aesthetic links are continuing with a new European project called *Let's Dance*.

We are convinced that real networking of this nature is the way forward for schools. There is so much to learn by working with people from different backgrounds and cultures, as was the case when the head teacher and assistant Head ran a four-day workshop in Athens. The Melina Mercouri Foundation funded the workshop and there were at least twenty different countries represented. Artists, educators and policy makers had time to work together, and to reflect on their practice. More important, even though everyone went back to their own countries, their partnership continues through a pan-European project called *Mimesis* and all concerned are still in touch through the Internet. The schools have also held a second meeting in Greece, with the aim of further networking of creative cultures, always with the key principles in mind: collaboration, communication, critical thinking, creativity and computers.

Of course, not everything at Richmond Park involves computers; a sixth C could be the country dancing which is a popular activity, and has been taught to partners in the shadow of the Acropolis. The school has also been asked by the Melina Mercouri Foundation to work with a theatre company from Turin in Italy, a secondary school from Lisle in France, and schools in Greece to explore the link between myth and drama. A further development has been the Radio Richmond project, which aims to take the school into new areas of ICT use. However, it is through the use of ICT and the Internet that we have been able to widen our pupils' understanding of their immediate environment and the wider world beyond.

Summary

- Our key principles are a shared vision, an emphasis on creative staff development and constant awareness of the progression of skills.
- The five Cs of a successful project are collaboration, communication, critical thinking, creativity and computers.
- Be happy, be a learner!

Part III

Policy and management issues

Chapter 10

Making broadband special

Chris Abbott

Watching Rapture, one of the youth-oriented cable television channels available in the UK, provides one example of the convergence between technologies which has been much predicted but is now finally a reality. During part of the day Rapture shows music videos which take up only part of the screen. A section below is reserved for text messages, which can be sent in real time to an e-mail address or by mobile phone text messaging. In this way, television viewers can communicate with each other and comment on the video currently showing. In the same way, the Internet is beginning to look more and more like a television channel. During the first phase of its existence, in the 1990s, it was a textual environment with an increasing number of images. By the end of the 1990s that had changed, with the effect that the Web had become a moving, changing, noisy and often confusing place where stillness and permanence are seldom to be found.

This trend is linked with other developments in on-line literacy; much of the media change seen in recent years is in the area described (Lanham 1994) as the 'icon–alphabet ratio'. Where once a message would have appeared mostly in text with a minimum of signs, it is now just as likely to be conveyed through images, with text playing a lesser or supportive role. This is a trend which has interested socio-linguists, and has been discussed at length in Kress and van Leuween (1996). Kress has considered the move to the iconic and symbolic across a range of media, including newspapers and other print products. Others, especially Snyder (1998, 2002) have focussed in particular on the changes that have taken place in digital environments and on computer screens, developing practices which Snyder describes in her latest book as 'silicon literacies'.

Part of the reason for this change has been the urge to push the technology to its limits, to give in to what has been described (Abbott 2001,

2002) as 'technological aestheticism'. The main driving force for the increase in sound and video, however, has been the move towards broadband rather than slower connections. When the Internet first became available in homes, schools and libraries, it was usually accessed through the telephone line, with a modem burbling away as it linked telephone with personal computer. For several years in the late 1980s and early 1990s modem technology was able to advance regularly, and faster connections became possible through this very simple technology.

By the mid-1990s governments and home users were looking to faster connections than are possible through normal telephone lines. A number of different systems have developed, usually known by a series of ever more bewildering acronyms. Whether the technology in use is ADSL or ISDN, whether the phone wire involved is made of copper or fibre-optic, and whether the connection is through a telephone or a television, the key to commercial success seems to be the offering of a faster connection.

Much of this has been driven by those who seek to make money from the Internet, whether it be through on-line commerce and sales or the less socially acceptable areas of on-line life such as gambling and pornography. These commercial drivers have been the source of much development in this area. Faster access and the availability of sound and video can be used in socially acceptable ways too, however, and schools will need to consider the issues that arise. Many of these are linked with previous concerns, for example regarding photographs and names, but others may be new.

It is not an insignificant decision to add sound or video to a school Web site. Both of these take up large amounts of storage space, and the host of the school Web site may set limits which will rule out large sound or video files. There are many problems to be solved regarding accessibility in this area, and site owners will need to be careful to ensure that they do not rule out access by previous users of their site when they add such new facilities. Both sound and video have appeared on Web sites first as incidental music or brief animations, but they have now begun to offer rather more interesting possibilities. Each will be considered in turn.

Sound

In the early days, the Internet was an apparently silent place. Sounds could be transmitted, but often needed to be downloaded first, taking many long minutes, before they could be played on the computer.

I remember one Christmas day downloading some jokey music on to a newly purchased computer; it took forty-five minutes to download the track but only two minutes to play it back. The same music is probably available now on a thousand Web sites, with almost instantaneous streamed playback as soon as a surfer lands on the site.

Streamed audio is the key to this development. Rather than the whole music track having to be downloaded before it is played back, only a part needs to be transferred; playback can then begin at the same time as the rest of the track is being processed. As is so often the case with technologies, there are a number of proprietary standards in this area, and users may need to install a range of software such as Real Player, Quicktime and Windows Media Player in order to hear the audio. It has become common for the basic versions of these players to be free, although they may need to be downloaded regularly. Publishing audio on the Web, rather than listening to it, is a much more expensive business and may involve purchasing software or moving to a more expensive Web host.

At first, audio was used very much as an incidental soundtrack. Visitors to a site were treated to an endlessly looping Muzak track which was only marginally less irritating than that heard on automated phone systems, although at least on the Web it could be turned off. Gradually people discovered more interesting uses of streamed audio. In particular, radio stations realised that whole new audiences were possible through this technology. Many local stations in countries such as the United States now transmit at least some of their programmes through the Web, and expatriates can tune in and keep up with developments at home. It is no surprise that the BBC, with its long history of worldwide broadcasting through the World Service, has made its news broadcasts and many of its most popular programmes available in this way, either simultaneously with their UK broadcast or as audio on demand.

This is as much a threat as an opportunity for the commercial sector, of course, as the Napster phenomenon indicated. The Napster system allowed people to exchange digitised music which they had stored on their computers with everyone else who registered. It was then easy to search for a particular track and download it. In many ways, this is the twenty-first-century equivalent of the development that followed the arrival of the blank audio cassette in the 1960s. For the first time, young people could cheaply record on cassette the tracks their friends might have in their record collections. Disapproval followed from the music companies which owned the copyright, but they were able to keep such recording manageable by their ability to create new and better standards of sound on original recordings. For many years the compact disc (CD) also worked to the advantage of the music companies, since it was difficult for a home user to record on to CD.

Digital sound, on the other hand, is extremely threatening to music companies, since it is easily copyable and duplicates are of exactly the same standard as the original. It was for this reason that the Napster system was eventually shut down, since it clearly infringed copyright law in many countries as well as threatening the profits of international music companies. Easy exchange of high-quality digital sound has not gone away, however, and this is an area which will receive much attention from lawyers and others in the near future.

Video

Video has followed a similar though rather slower development pattern, since the storage and processing power required to handle video is even greater than that needed for audio. Limited at first to looping animated icons, movement on screen gradually developed from the fringes to the main menu areas itself. A Web site which might have been a static silent place a few years ago is now likely to be introduced by a movie sequence clearly influenced by feature film trailers, and menu items will change as the mouse nears them, or sounds will be used to attract the surfer. An example of a large commercial site which has done this is the official *Harry Potter* Web site (harrypotter.warnerbros.com).

Broadcast video has joined broadcast audio on the Web, as streaming technology can deliver video in the same way as it does audio. News broadcasts are available anywhere in the world almost at the moment they are shown in the originating country. Clips of television programmes are offered to surfers, although not usually the whole programme for copyright reasons. Some film makers are beginning to see the Web as a means of getting greater audiences for their films, especially as Webcasting may later lead viewers to see their projects in cinemas or on television. Most major feature film trailers are now available on the Web. The development of Flash technology, another plug-in for Web browsers, has provided a new animation medium to set alongside drawn or cel animation, stop-motion or sand tray. Online Flash animation festivals have begun to appear, and galleries of short films are increasing rapidly (www.atomfilms.com).

Symbols

The new swimming pool in Kemi, a small town in northern Finland, is an impressive place in many ways. It manages to combine sleek modern steel, glass and wood architecture with a high degree of comfort and functionality for its users. The same could be said of many municipal swimming pools, of course, but at Kemi customer care has also extended to ensuring that the needs of symbol users are met.

Throughout the swimming pool complex, symbols are used not just as signposts to facilities but as points of reference and reminders next to particular locations. The symbols are from the Pictogram set, commonly used in Finland and some of the other Nordic countries. When arriving for a swim, a symbol user will see Pictograms in every part of the complex: the changing rooms, the cash desk and even the café. These symbols are not merely signs that take the place of textual pointers; they illustrate the use of facilities such as showers and locker rooms, or provide support for user choice, for example, when a symbolised menu is offered in the café instead of the text-based one.

Figure 10.1 Pictogram for a shower

Figure 10.2 Pictogram for a sauna

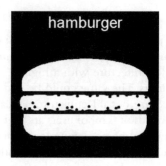

Figure 10.3 Pictogram for a hamburger

The Kemi swimming pool has an extensive Web site, which is also available in English (http://www.kemi.fi/Uimahalli/english). Unfortunately the Web site does not, at the time of writing, include a symbol-enhanced section, although it seems likely that it will do so in the future in view of the centre's serious commitment to the needs of symbol users.

The Internet has opened up a range of new possibilities for people with special needs who make use of symbols, especially where symbol-based Web sites have been developed, and as e-mail through symbols becomes possible. There will be an increasing need for public places to become as symbol-literate as the Kemi swimming pool. As has been pointed out, 'Many young people are emerging from education "symbol literate" and expect to be able to continue this means of communication' (Detheridge 2000: 2).

The development of symbol use within special needs has been described elsewhere (Abbott 2000; Detheridge and Detheridge 1997; Detheridge 2000) and the emphasis here will be on the extent to which symbol communication and literacy can be said to be part of Internet life. This is an area which has begun to interest linguists and others who seek to document changing literacies (Abbott 2002). Although their use antedates the Internet, and indeed the personal computer, symbolised resources have been revolutionised by ICT. Before the availability of symbol processors and other ICT-based tools, it was necessary to draw symbols or photocopy them and then cut them out to make resources. Most symbol users now use a program such as Writing with Symbols 2000 (Widgit 2000) to speed up these activities and to ensure consistency and appropriateness of resources.

The use of symbols has been of great importance to many young people, as has been suggested elsewhere.

The capacity of symbols to bypass many of the problems normally associated with the written word has afforded access for many children with special educational needs to a broader range of learning opportunities than they had previously known. In turn, this has led to greater autonomy. Children who may never have read through the previous means available to us have now been helped into that learning domain so valuable for life.

(Detheridge and Detheridge 1997: vi)

The Widgit Web site (http://www.widgit.com) contains more information about *Writing with Symbols 2000* (WWS2000), and also provides links to a changing collection of symbol resources which can be accessed on-line. At the time of writing these included, for example, a large list of links to sites dealing with alternative and augmentative communication (AAC) and symbols, as well as links to some of the sites developed by other special needs resource and support organisations. Subject resources are being developed too, including an extensive symbolised information bank dealing with rain forests.

There are complex decisions associated with symbol use, and an attempt to define the key issues (Abbott 2000) resulted in a range of

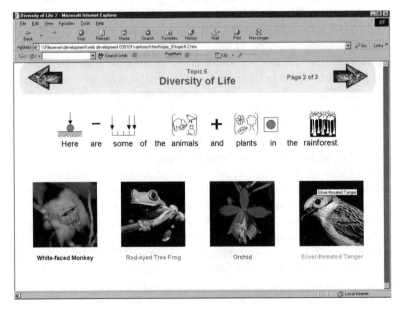

Figure 10.4 Part of the rain-forest resource from Widgit

topics being identified. Symbols can be used for very different purposes, and all of these raise issues related to vocabulary, consistency and understanding. Communication with symbols may be different in its constituent parts and in the approaches needed from the use of symbols to support literacy. Symbols can also be used to enable users to access information, and to become more included within educational and other settings. Unfortunately, much of the evidence related to symbol use is difficult to locate and may be anecdotal; it is important that users, carers and teachers should be encouraged to document their activities. This has begun to happen (Hooker and Sullivan 2000, 2001) and it is to be hoped that the trend will continue. In his articles describing the review process and AAC from a user's point of view, Hooker reminds agencies involved in those areas of the importance of symbol use, on-line and elsewhere.

Most on-line development of symbols to date has been linked with Web sites, making those sites accessible to a wider range of potential users. Schools were among the pioneers in this area, with Meldreth Manor (www.meldrethmanor.com) often mentioned, quite rightly, in this context. Other schools have begun to develop symbol-based sites, and David Fettes describes in Chapter 3 the ways in which he did just this at Mandeville School (www.mandeville.ealing.sch.uk) in west London.

Other resource providers have been a little slower at providing symbolised access through their sites, and it seems likely that this is related to being unaware of the need rather than to any conscious decision to rule out this particular group of users. As Carolyn Howitt and Jodi Mattes show in Chapter 4, it is essential that the needs of special users are considered early in the process of developing a resource site for a major institution such as a national museum. Other providers may well be able to add symbolised and other special access at a later stage.

It has recently become possible for symbol users to send e-mail to each other without having to be able to access text. The most straight-forward way of doing this is by the use of another add-on program developed by the Writing with Symbols team and known as Inter_Comm (Widgit 2001). With the address book shown as a set of photographs and automatic translation between different symbol sets, this is adding a significant new channel of communication to those available to people who use this form of communication. Because WWS2000 is used in many different countries and languages, e-mail communication across geographical and linguistic barriers is also possible.

The possibilities are exciting, and the next few years will see rapid development in this area, not just on the part of users but also among those who are interested in researching and supporting this area. At the moment the potential has been recognised for the most part by those organisations which support special needs users of the Internet, including Ability Net (www.abilitynet.co.uk) and the WAACIS Project (www.waacis.org.uk). WAACIS hopes to gain funding to expand its work and train many more special needs users to access the Internet; if this expansion goes ahead, there are likely to be a great many more users of the on-line symbol-based tools that are developing.

As Detheridge and Detheridge pointed out several years ago:

> Once people have found their voice it is almost impossible to take it away. Those instances which have given us most pleasure, seeing children involved in the curriculum without the frustration of not being able to read and write text; a parent in tears when their 12 year old brought something home for the first time that he could read . . . – all these should become more and more commonplace as children and adults with learning disabilities come to take a more active role in society.
>
> (Detheridge and Detheridge 1997: 126)

Symbols have done so much through previous media; the Internet offers even more in the way of possibilities, provided that resource providers recognise the need to include symbol users in their projected audiences and to plan accordingly.

Issues for inclusion

What, then, are the issues here for the teacher or administrator seeking to make use of faster Internet access to promote and support inclusion? In many ways, the audio and video possibilities described, and the increase in speed of access that makes them possible, do not change the menu so much as make more of it accessible or achieveable. Just as children's writing and artwork have appeared on school Web sites, so can their musical compositions or animated sequences – or even short video films.

Sound is a more straightforward proposition than video, and the traps and concerns are fewer and less dramatic in their outcome. Parental permission will certainly be needed before a student's voice is published on a Web site, at least if it is identified rather than left anonymous, but musical compositions can be made available without safety concerns. Point-to-point voice calls, however, or audio chat, should be treated with the same caution as a telephone call. If you would not allow pupils to go to the school office and telephone someone at random – and presumably few of us would do so – then you should not allow them unsupervised access to on-line audio connectivity. Booked calls to known partners are quite another issue, however, and it seems likely that audio links will develop most effectively as an extension of the sort of e-mail projects described by David Ware in Chapter 7.

Video is far more complex and fraught with difficulty. Much current use of streaming video capability has been linked, directly or indirectly, with the pornography and allied industries. Most open on-line video-chat environments are entirely unsuitable for minors to access, or for use within an educational environment. Web-based video conferencing is still perfectly acceptable, however, if it takes place point-to-point, with a known partner, and is arranged beforehand. This is relatively easy to set up, as most of the Web-based video-conferencing programs make use of the unique identifying number, the IP number, attached to each computer accessing the Internet. By calling the number previously advised to you by your partner, you can be sure that you will connect with that institution and no other. There is a small complication in some cases, as your Internet service provider (ISP) may give you a different IP number each time you log on, rather than allocating one to you permanently. However, this is more often a problem with ISPs servicing the home market than it is within education. If you are faced with this difficulty, simply log on, check the number you have been allocated, and e-mail it to your partner, who will then be able to call you. It is vital for video-conferencing projects to take place only with trusted partners. Any recordings of the video chat should be made for use in the two institutions only and not placed on either school's Web site.

There are clearly some major issues here, and it would be tempting to say it is safer simply to have nothing to do with video-conferencing, but to do so would be to turn our back on a tool which has vast poten-tial. If your pupils enjoy contacting a partner school by voice call, why deny a deaf student the chance to join in by signing across a video link? The present picture quality is only just good enough to send video of signing, but this will improve rapidly. The ability to participate fully in a video-conference conversation will be a routine twenty-first-century skill, and all young people should be able to develop their expertise with this technology. School is the appropriate place for it to begin.

Summary

- The Web, once composed of text and still images, now offers sound, animation and video.
- Convergence of telephone, television and computer is becoming a reality.
- Fast Internet connections offer particular benefits for learners with special educational needs.
- Symbol users, in particular, have much to gain from an image-enhanced Internet.

References

Abbott, C. (ed.) (2000) *Symbols Now*, Leamington Spa: Widgit Software.

Abbott, C. (2001) 'Some young male Web site owners: the technological aesthete, the community builder and the professional activist', *Education, Communication and Information* 1 (2), 197–212.

Abbott, C. (2002) 'Writing the visual: the use of graphic symbols in on-screen texts' in I. Snyder (ed.), *Silicon Literacies: Education, Communication and New Technologies*, London: Routledge.

Detheridge, M., and Detheridge, T. (1997) *Literacy through Symbols: Improving Access for Children and Adults*, London: David Fulton.

Detheridge, T. (ed.) (2000) *Introduction to Symbols*, Leamington Spa: Widgit Software.

Hooker, M., and Sullivan, J. (2000) 'Creating a culture of understanding', *Community Living* 13 (4), 16–17.

Hooker, M., and Sullivan, J. (2001) 'Whose review is it anyway?' *Community Living* 14 (3), 16–17.

Kress, G., and Leeuwen, T. van (1996) *Reading Images: The Grammar of Visual Design*, London: Routledge.

Lanham, R. (1994) *The Electronic Word: Democracy, Technology, and the Arts*, Chicago: University of Chicago Press.

Snyder, I. (ed.) (1998) *Page to Screen: Taking Literacy into the Electronic Era*, London: Routledge.

Snyder, I. (ed.) (2002) *Silicon Literacies: Education, Communication and the New Technologies*, London: Routledge.

Widgit (2000) *Writing with Symbols 2000*, Leamington Spa: Widgit Software.

Widgit (2001) *Inter_Comm*, Leamington Spa: Widgit Software.

Chapter 11

A passion for excellence

Mel Farrar

From his perspective as the head teacher of a special school, Mel Farrar explains how Internet use at his school has arisen from previous activities. He also shows how the Internet can be used to raise a school's profile and to ensure that its aims are understood by the agencies and users with which it is connected.

Communication is central to any organisation, as Foxdenton School has found during the twenty-eight years it has existed. Internet use at Foxdenton is a natural extension of what has gone before, where 'structuring success' and 'aiming for excellence' are key concepts. The school Web site is an important part of this philosophy. Foxdenton is a state primary school purpose-built in 1973 for up to 120 children aged between 2 and 11 years with special educational needs (SEN) arising from physical or medical difficulties. It has an integrated nursery which brings together pupils with and without special needs. The school offers many services in conjunction with the local Health Service trust.

When it opened in 1973 Foxdenton was a new school, making provision for a group of youngsters who were being enabled to live by rapid advances in medical science. These children needed a range of medical and paramedical help, and many had a tentative hold on life: but for the first time they were able to attend a day school within their own community. There were no clear precedents for such a school but the original governors (one of whom is still with the school today as chairman), the head teacher and staff had a clear customer focus and set out to provide, within the state sector, the best possible service to pupils and parents. We talked of 'aiming not merely to satisfy but to delight'. From the outset we also aimed for clarity of vision and purpose: no less than a thirty-year plan, in fact.

Putting the child at the heart of the process, the early touchstones for the pupils were structuring success and building self-esteem. The whole team applied themselves to that end, melding their diverse skills and professional backgrounds. Within the classroom and in therapy this meant positive, challenging intervention and support, and outside the classroom we grew a whole host of extracurricular activities like Cubs, Brownies, swimming and drama clubs, some led by child-care staff. This philosophy also meant identifying needs, exploring new approaches to teaching and therapy, introducing and sometimes designing new technology to aid communication, mobility or control of the environment, and a whole range of activities for pupils within and outside the normal day. The aim was to ensure that they came willingly to school and that each day was full and fulfilled, exciting, challenging and happy.

The notion of 'children first' gave us a rationale for prioritising our activities and channelling our energies; going the extra mile became a way of life. In the 1980s, fired by the ideas of Tom Peters (Peters and Waterman 1982, 1985), we readily embraced the notion of learning from the people you serve, and found that, if you set out to understand and meet their needs, you really can trust the customer. Between

Aiming for Excellence

Figure 11.1 The Foxdenton school Web site, showing awards

1984 and 1986 we introduced monthly newsletters, annual parental surveys, whole-school planning and review systems and an innovative staff development policy. Though we did not characterise it as such at the time, we intuitively began to shape up four principles which have been of profound importance in relation to our stakeholders: inform, involve, empower and recognise. In the 1990s, backed by a skilled and stable team, we sought out and engaged with all the major quality systems in the public sector: OFSTED, the EFQM Excellence® Model, Investors in People, Charter Mark, ISO and Service Excellence Awards, among others. Though not in thrall to them we have found that each can add a new layer of insight to our work as we have looked for and achieved improvement year on year.

Our home page at once exemplifies and reflects our approach. It exemplifies our approach because, in our determination to seek further continuing improvements, the advances in communication technology were too important to be overlooked. For our pupils' sake we also had to explore and exploit its possibilities. The site reflects the fact that this approach has enabled us to stay ahead of the field in customer satisfaction and yielded significant external recognition.

The use of the Internet in school

We were very fortunate in our resources for taking forward Internet use within Foxdenton. We had a teacher whose focus since 1981 had been technology and switch development, and who spent hours of her own time mastering the field and bringing the benefit of her work to the children. One of our two deputies was an early exponent of the use of technology for administrative use, especially finance. In 1994 a young man came to us straight from university as a volunteer with an HND in Information Technology, and made himself so invaluable that he created his own job as Deputy Administrator. Because of the nature of our youngsters' needs, we had good links with the SEMERC Centre and later the ACE Access Centre, both organisations responsible for matching technology to the needs of learners. Finally a healthy school fund meant that we were not bound entirely by the budget.

In looking at the growing importance of the Internet in our special school there are two strands: one relates to the pupils and the other to the organisation. Although both are important, other chapters in this book effectively highlight the value of the Internet to pupils: here we touch on this, but focus more on the external agenda and, in particular, our Web site. With the expansion of Beacon Schools, databases, Best

Practice Web sites and more entrepreneurial activity at school level we see that agenda continuing to grow in importance.

Pupils

Many of our pupils come to us with physical, medical or learning difficulties which restrict their opportunities. From a very early stage we sought out technology which would give them increasing control over their environment and access to the world of learning. The earliest electric typewriters came in useful for some youngsters; later we used the enormous Possum machines which enabled recording and environmental control through a cursor mechanism. A great deal of effort went into developing switches to increase access and then programs, especially on the early BBC machines, which could build on these. With the advent of the Internet these switches could be used to access the wider world of information, and this was taken forward through a grant from the National Grid for Learning, which gave us an Internet point in every department, though not every classroom, in the school.

Pupils were enthusiastic about the use of this new tool and it was the focus of a joint project funded as a pilot by the New Opportunities Fund. This project was an after-school computer club which brought together Foxdenton School with pupils from another special school and a nearby mainstream school (Mason *et al.* 1999). The grant also incorporated the Foxdenton-based Club for Gifted Mathematicians from across Oldham, which found some interesting contacts through the World Wide Web.

Internet access and use fulfil many of the aims of the school. These include broadening horizons, giving responsibility, developing autonomy, building self-esteem and of course structuring success: and it was not long before we took the decision to build our own Web site. With a growing national profile we were able to secure sponsorship from the Oldham-based special needs software company, Inclusive Technology. They gave us access to their Web builder and advice on the development of the site, with their expertise used to incorporate our ideas. We have also made good use of volunteers and students to help in preparation of materials for and improvements to the site – these have included sixth-form students and also university students pursuing a degree in Quality Management (part of the considerable range of voluntary help we attract each year). A big advantage of the Web is the ability to develop and produce work off-site through the use of e-mail. For a period our Web builder worked in Sweden and that did not prove a problem, although it is nice to have face-to-face contact occasionally.

In terms of our four principles one could see that, together, the Internet and Web site have become another important tool in our armoury as pupils are increasingly:

- *Informed* – information coming in; use in topic work, in planning visits, finding out about events and (royal) visitors to school; Web site pictures of the work of classmates, access to pupils in other settings within and outside school, and links with past pupils.
- *Involved* – in the virtual tour, in preparing material, in building and sharing their ideas; in joint integrated activities where physical restrictions are not significant.
- *Empowered* – switch access for children with physical difficulties tools, e-mails; an intranet (more to do to develop this, but worth the effort).
- *Recognised* – Web site pictures of children and their work; roll of honour from the monthly newsletter, minutes of the school council meeting; structuring success and building self-esteem.

Organisation and communication

In developing systems to ensure delivery of an outstanding service to pupils and parents we needed to know who our stakeholders were and how we could improve our links with them and knowledge about them. In this the EFQM Excellence® model offered us some important pointers (Lloyds TSB 2001). Figure 11.2 sets out, within the framework of the model (which can valuably be used for any organisation), the key stakeholders of Foxdenton. The chart has many uses, but in this analysis we see how widespread can be the impact of the Internet. Hardly any are left untouched by our communications, and links with almost all can be enhanced with better communications.

As the first school in Oldham to install a fax machine (as recently as 1990) it was natural that we should want to be ahead of the field when the Internet offered speedier communication, and especially when there was the opportunity for interactivity.

Our newsletters have been produced monthly since 1985 with up to thirty double-sided pages, lots of photographs and regular sections covering the Head's editorial; news about children's activities, curricular and extracurricular; Staff Reporter, parents' pages, roll of honour and thanks pages. The newsletters have played a vital role in managing our

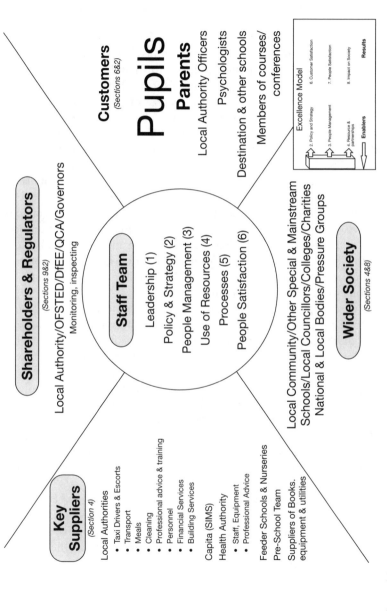

Key Suppliers
(Section 4)

Local Authorities
- Taxi Drivers & Escorts
- Transport
- Meals
- Cleaning
- Professional advice & training
- Personnel
- Financial Services
- Building Services

Capita (SIMS)

Health Authority
- Staff, Equipment
- Professional Advice

Feeder Schools & Nurseries

Pre-School Team

Suppliers of Books, equipment & utilities

Shareholders & Regulators
(Sections 9&2)

Local Authority/OFSTED/DfEE/QCA/Governors

Monitoring, inspecting

Staff Team

Leadership (1)
Policy & Strategy (2)
People Management (3)
Use of Resources (4)
Processes (5)
People Satisfaction (6)

Customers
(Sections 6&2)

Pupils

Parents

Local Authority Officers

Psychologists

Destination & other schools

Members of courses/conferences

Excellence Model

	6. Customer Satisfaction
2. Policy and Strategy	
3. People Management	7. People Satisfaction
4. Resource & partnerships	8. Impact on Society
Enablers	**Results**

Wider Society
(Sections 4&8)

Local Community/Other Special & Mainstream Schools/Local Councillors/Colleges/Charities National & Local Bodies/Pressure Groups

Figure 11.2 Stakeholders at Foxdenton

constituency. Initially the target audience was parents, and they still remain the main focus, but as we have better understood our stakeholders and found much wider interest in our activities the audience has increased.

Newsletters are used to highlight children's activities and celebrate their successes, to signal and record events in school, to consult on, adumbrate or explain policy, and to inform and acknowledge those who help us. They are valuable in ensuring that the school is close to the customer even if we are two hours away by bus. A copy goes to all parents, members of staff, governors, key officers, psychologists, medical consultants and fund raisers in Oldham and the other boroughs that send us pupils, and is available for drivers and escorts, visitors and prospective parents. For 120 pupils we do a run of 350 and there is often a need for extra copies. With a regional intake drawing from a population of 600,000, there is no local newspaper and, apart from the national media (on which we have featured from time to time), no one radio or television station which can carry our news. Hence our newsletters seek to reach all parents and key officers and personnel (including some councillors) in the authorities from which we draw. From our communication matrix we can see that the Web site is a natural development of our work in the area of communication.

Increasingly the Web site has become the front door of the school, where impressions are formed before any formal contact has been made. It is therefore very important that those impressions are good ones. The medium may be new but the principle is not; we have always been aware that for many parents impressions of the school are formed or created by people other than our own staff. However professional or friendly we may appear when we greet people on the phone or on a visit, they will often have a half or fully formed view of us before we even talk to them. Prospective parents meet others in hospital clinics or community groups. They are seeking information often ahead of ringing us, or grandparents or neighbours will make enquiries on parents' behalf through their own Web of contacts.

It was this realisation which impelled our drive for good communications and for sharing the whole story with our parents, staff and governors so that they were better briefed and had positive images to convey. Clearly, the Web site has a role to play in extending the audience whilst cutting down the cost of communication.

Feedback

In seeking to improve the service we had to include feedback in the structure. At pupil level this came through reviews, comments on reports and more recently the in-house focus group of the school council. Parents give us feedback through the daily home/school books, in annual reviews (where an opening question is always 'What are you pleased with and what concerns do you have?'), on annual reports and particularly through the parental survey. This last has been an immensely important tool in evaluating the effectiveness of and satisfaction with our communications and services. It affirms the positive and identifies scope for improvement.

The results include anonymised comments from reports, and these are widely circulated, in the original wording, in a publication called *Parent Voices*. Since the aim is to share our values and our success in meeting our aims, the Web site is a natural extension of the audience for this publication. With the advent of the Web site we can strengthen our feedback, as it encourages contact with an even wider group and we often get messages from grandparents or other relatives across the world through our guest book. In 1999 we introduced a home/school agreement setting out in one document what our customers could expect from us. It was drawn up with major help from our parent governors and then a draft was included in our newsletter and published on our Web site asking for further comments.

Place of the Web site

We believe that sharing information is empowering to all concerned. Some see power as a four-foot post; others as a willow tree. In the first model any information given away reduces the power at the centre. We believe in the empowerment which comes from giving people the information and trusting them to use it. It is true that such information can be used negatively, but our experience has been almost always positive and, with a much greater pay-off, worth the risk. Within our community and beyond it we have found nothing to fear in making information widely available. What we have noticed is that computer ownership takes an unusual pattern, where (like cable or satellite television) it is not limited to certain groups or reflective of economic status. It thus reaches people who would not normally read our other communications.

For parents as well as children the Internet can be used to ensure they are:

- *Informed* – the parents' page on the Web site features the prospectus, surveys, information about the school, newsletter headings, governors' report to parents and annual meeting; the service and resource directory. Much more is available through the other pages.
- *Involved* – the school seeking feedback on the home/school agreement; we have had e-mails from prospective parents, highlighting their concerns and interests.
- *Empowered* – through the opportunity for feedback; *Parent Voices*; nursery survey; opening up the school to give parents questions to ask. Knowledge is power – we believe in sharing it.
- *Recognised* – featuring the contribution of parents, for example through the Eco-school agenda, painting the parents' room; to their child as 'A Year in the life of Patrick'; roll of honour; published surveys and anonymised comments on reports; thanks page.

Taking a leaf out of the *Yellow Pages* book (*Yellow Pages* won the UK Quality Award in 1998, the year before ourselves) we drew up a list of all the people who had made an impact on our service: those who worked in the school and those who had helped us through partnerships, through sponsorship, through fund raising or through influence. This we published in our newsletter and on the Web site.

Similar considerations apply to staff and other stakeholders, and a visit to our site will show that we have taken these groups into consideration in designing our pages. A number of our past pupils comprise a community of people who, in many cases for health reasons, are not able to hold down full-time positions or are home-bound. They have shown that they want to be part of our network and share in the school's successes and developments.

What is on the Web site?

- *Location*
  A plan of the school
  How to reach us – physically and virtually, with a map and e-mail contact addresses
  A virtual tour led by pupils
- *Pupil pages*
  Meet our pupils
  Club activities
  Children's projects
  Computer Club, Gifted Mathematicians' Club

This month's roll of honour
- *Staff pages*
  Meet our staff
  Staff projects
  Staff pictures/awards
  National training award
  Services and resources directory
- *Parents' pages*
  Annual parental survey
  Prospectus; services for parents
  Home/school agreement
  Annual report to parents
- *Governors' pages*
  Meet our governors
  Governors' annual report
- *News and newsletters; Health Service partners; Oldham Metropolitan Borough Council*
- *Our journey to excellence*
  Quality models, quality tools and Foxdenton best practice ideas
  Copies of submissions for some awards
  Foxdenton Ventures: presentations, conferences, consultancy and Training
- *Feedback page*
  How we can improve our Web site?
  What else do people want to see?

Whereas most schools will now have many features similar to the above, we believe that we have gone further than most in being open about our school and in sharing what we do and have done with the widest possible audience. Our passion for excellence is no mere introspective activity; we do want to spread the word about the benefits of trusting the customer. As winners of a European Quality Prize, and several other accolades along the way, we feel we have a responsibility to share our work with the wider public. We aim to do so not simply through presenting at conferences, which can be extremely expensive for delegates, but by making our ideas accessible across the World Wide Web. We have found significant interest in our quality journey among professionals across Europe and have set up a number of mutually beneficial partnerships. Not all are from education: many are from the commercial sector, and some of our best practice ideas have been picked up by companies such as Littlewoods and TNT.

It was for this reason that we developed the 'Our journey to excellence' page. Echoing the front page, this section has on it the logos of awards which we have won and behind each an explanation of what the award entails, together with some feedback from the assessors on our service. In most cases there is a link to the Web site of the host organisation, which can be used to fill out the background to the award and enable interested parties to take it further. Where appropriate we have been willing to share our winning submissions, or extracts from them, as that provides a starting point for those who wish to explore or embark on their own quality journey. Clicking on the Charter Mark logo gives our winning submission for the 2000 Charter Mark and is accompanied by the assessor's full feedback report. Together they provide a very good platform for public sector organisations interested in improving their customer focus.

The 'Journey to excellence' page is backed up by a 'Quality tools' page, which shares some of the tools we have developed along the way. This replicates the parental survey, and offers a blank version which people can download for their own use. The page also reproduces some articles and presentations, now an increasingly popular way of saving paper and ensuring that those who want to know (and make the effort) receive the appropriate material. The usefulness of this page was underlined when a Head from Gloucestershire rang out of the blue. Our school had been mentioned in conversation and he wanted to follow it up. He was planning a Staff Development Day, and in a twenty-minute conversation we were able to provide background information on the excellence model, a staff consultation exercise, a parental survey template, and a plan of campaign: all the materials were available on and could be downloaded from the site.

There is always more to do, always room for improvement and innovation. Last year the site was used for advertising an international special needs conference, with booking forms and updated information on the programme and joining instructions. There will be an increasing focus on a marketing function as the school develops more material or services which people want to purchase, for example our Literacy Hour video, or the Christmas musical. The next step is to develop a vehicle for the training and consultancy arm of the school through a not-for-profit trust: Foxdenton Ventures. In this the Web site will play a key role.

Since we set up our site less than two years ago Foxdenton has enjoyed unprecedented success. That is not purely a result of using the Internet, but it has clearly helped, and our Web site would certainly have damned us had it not been a little better than ordinary. Rooted in outstanding customer satisfaction, that success has come in all the major quality standards for the public sector: the UK Business Excellence Award; the European Quality Prize, Investors in People, Charter Mark, a Unisys Service Excellence award, an Eco-school Award and a School Achievement Award. Foxdenton has also been included in the Vision 100 index of the UK's most visionary organisations and, as a case study, in a number of government publications.

Summary

Our formula includes:

- a strong customer focus;
- a bias for action;
- a can-do mind-set;
- the involvement of all our stakeholders in planning;
- an evaluative culture with effective and comprehensive feedback and review procedures;
- extensive and up-beat communications;
- a drive for continuous improvement.

This formula is nothing to do with Foxdenton being a special school. It draws on principles and systems which, enthusiastically applied, would make any school – indeed, any organisation – special. Translated into a school context, that formula embraces:

- high expectations to raise achievement in children;
- partnership with parents and key stakeholders;
- a premium on staff development and empowerment;
- emphasis on success and an inclusive approach;
- links with the community;
- a team approach which includes parents, staff, governors, volunteers, the authorities and the community;
- an overarching passion for excellence.

Involving, informing, empowering and recognising the Internet has proved an amazingly effective tool.

References

Cabinet Office (2001) 'The Foxdenton case study' in *Getting it Together: A Guide to Quality Schemes and the Delivery of Public Services*, London: HMSO.

Farrar, M. R., Keegan, G., O'Connell, B., Rowlands, K., Steed, C. and Pupius, M. (2001) *The Excellence Model in Education*, Chichester: Kingsham Press.

Farrar M. R. (1991) 'Close to the customer: a *modus supervivendi* for the special school' in Bower (ed.) *Schools, Services and Special Educational Needs: Management Issues in the Wake of LMSS*, Cambridge: Perspective Press.

Farrar M. R. (1992) 'Close to the customer', *Primary Health Care Management* 2 (12), 7–8.

Farrar M. R. (2000) 'Structuring success: a case study in the use of the EFQM® excellence model in school improvement', *Total Quality Management* 11 (4–5), S 691–6.

Farrar M. R., and Crabtree, H. (1999) 'Achieving customer loyalty in an educational market place', *Total Quality Management* 10 (4–5), S 531–9.

Lloyds TSB (2001) *Quality in Education: School Self-assessment using the Excellence Model*, Bristol: Lloyds Quality Team.

Parry, M. (1999) *The Submission Writer's Handbook*, 2nd edn, Bristol: Bristol Quality Centre.

Peters T., and Waterman R. (1982) *In Search of Excellence*, New York: Random House.

Peters T., and Waterman, R. (1985) *A Passion for Excellence*, New York: Random House.

Chapter 12

Supporting SEN teachers
Policy and management issues

Chris Stevens and Terry Waller

Chris Stevens and Terry Waller have much experience of supporting teachers and local education authorities (LEAs) in the use of technology for inclusion. Based on their work at BECTA, they discuss national developments in the UK and the likely potential of newer technologies such as broadband technology and speech recognition.

Today there is a widely accepted view that ICT can have an impact on the way teaching and learning takes place in schools and that it can contribute to raising standards.

> Schools that have good ICT resources and use them well tended to have better standards than schools where good ICT resources are not well used . . .

> Schools that made good use of ICT to improve standards generally had high-quality teaching of ICT, a favourable school ethos in relation to ICT, good pupil access to ICT resources, high pupil ICT skills, and have developed in their pupils a positive attitude to ICT.
>
> (BECTA 2001: 8)

In particular it has been recognised that ICT can have specific benefits for the whole range of learners with special educational needs when used effectively. Indeed, for some learners it can provide a lifeline, enabling access to communication, education and the curriculum. However, reports from OFSTED (OFSTED 2001a, b) have indicated that ICT in special schools is often weak and, where pupils with special educational needs (SEN) are in mainstream schools, the use of ICT to support those pupils is also poor.

Teaching with ICT in special schools remains a weakness. Teachers continue to have problems identifying ICT resources to match the range of pupils' capabilities and curriculum needs.

(OFSTED 2001a: 3)

Pupils' achievements and the quality of teaching in ICT remain low. Pupils' achievement is lowest in information technology. Achievement is good in less than half and unsatisfactory in two in five schools, reflecting teachers' uncertainty with the effective use of ICT across other subjects as well as with teaching information technology.

(OFSTED 2001b: 56–7)

There appears to be a continuing gap between accepted wisdom and the reality of the classroom. This chapter explores some of the support that is available, in terms of policies that provide a clear framework of expectations in this area and in the provision of practical tools which, if well managed, should effect real change.

The current position

For years, initiatives have involved single elements of the three strands necessary to ensure really efficient integration of the use of ICT into the teaching and learning process: equipment, training or content. For the first time at the end of the last century there was recognition that all these elements need to come together, be championed by government and adopted as a whole of the educational sector. Denis Stevenson, in his report for the Labour Party in 1997, set out a vision of ICT in schools.

All young people – whether they have access to ICT at home or not – should be able to apply a basic confidence and competence in the use of ICT to all aspects of their learning experience.

Teachers in turn should be so confident and competent in the use of ICT that they are able to use it in all aspects of their daily work.

We wish to see a society within ten years where ICT has permeated the entirety of education (as it will the rest of society) so that it is no longer a talking point but taken for granted – rather as electricity has come to be.

(Stevenson 1997: 4)

The vision also recognised that ICT should be seen only as a tool for teachers, albeit a powerful one, and that no extravagant claims should be made for its potential unless it is mediated by skilled professionals.

> We want to emphasise that ICT is in no sense a substitute for 'traditional' learning and teaching. Nor is it a substitute for students using their minds and imaginations. The role of ICT is to serve education: in particular by helping students to learn more effectively and by helping teachers to do their professional job. Attempts are sometimes made to suggest that ICT is in some way the property of a particular educational philosophy. We do not see it that way. The best analogue we have heard for ICT is the analogue with the invention of electricity. Electricity – once regarded as a strange, almost frightening wonder of the age – has come to serve almost every aspect of society. So also with ICT. It should be used in the service of the curriculum, and made available to help teachers to manage the learning process, however that is defined by them.
>
> (Stevenson 1997: 4)

The report went on to list recommendations that influenced and shaped policy in this area. The government's aims were articulated in the form of a challenge to the key players that they identified as needing to engage in radically reforming the situation. This document, *Open for Learning, Open for Business*, also set a series of targets for education:

> As a Government we shall adopt the targets for Information and Communications Technology (ICT) in the learning society which we set out in the consultation paper. These include the following targets for 2002:
>
> • connecting all schools, colleges, universities, public libraries and as many community centres as possible to the Grid;
> • ensuring that serving teachers feel confident and are competent to teach using ICT within the curriculum; and that librarians are similarly trained;
> • enabling school leavers to have a good understanding of ICT, with measures in place for assessing their competence in it;
> • ensuring that general administrative communications between education bodies and the Government and its agencies cease to be largely paper-based;

• making Britain a centre for excellence in the development of networked software content, and a world leader in the export of learning services.

(DfEE 1998b: 6)

The report also presented the vision of a National Grid for Learning as both a structure of educationally valuable content on the Internet and a programme for developing the means to access that content in schools, libraries, colleges, universities, workplaces, homes and elsewhere. Funding was made available to support these targets. Between 1998 and 2004 the government committed over £1 billion of expenditure to improve schools' ICT facilities. The infrastructure, the wiring and equipment to provide schools with access to the Internet and to purchase content, was provided through the Standards Fund, a funding mechanism to support government priorities in education.

In 1999 the New Opportunities Fund set up a four-year programme, ICT Training for Teachers, School Librarians, and Public Librarians, that provided opportunities for all practising teachers and school librarians to undertake training in the use of ICT in the curriculum. This training, by approved training providers, aimed to ensure that teachers and school librarians are equipped with the necessary knowledge, understanding and skills to make sound decisions about when and how to use ICT effectively in teaching. There was also a programme to train public librarians in ICT. The training is intended to bring serving teachers up to the same level as newly qualified teachers (NQTs) and all training is required to address how technology supports pupils with special educational needs. The scheme also includes a range of trainers offering specialist SEN courses. The Teacher Training Agency (TTA) produced an *ICT Needs Identification* CD-ROM to support teachers in assessing their training needs. It enables them to consider their own skills in using ICT with pupils with a range of learning needs and illustrated how ICT can help pupils access the curriculum.

The development of the National Grid for Learning portal provided a mechanism for teachers and other to easily locate the best educational resources around. It is anticipated that with this scale of government investment content developers will provide high quality on-line resources that will engage the widest spectrum of learners. Additional funding also became available to test out higher-speed connections (broadband) and the development of content that could be delivered using this both over the Internet but also through digital television and other electronic devices.

Moving into the new millennium, the recognition that training needs to be an on-going process is central to government policy. This is not only in the area of ICT but also in that of developing a teaching profession that is able to support the full range of needs of pupils that are educated either in special schools or mainstream. The need for continuing professional development in specialist areas of SEN is reflected in the TTA *National Special Educational Needs Specialist Standards* (TTA 1999) and in a CD-ROM tool for teachers to use to assess their own skills and identify training and development needs.

SEN were seen very much as part of the NGfL developments. In designing the grid the consultation report emphasised that:

> The grid has the potential to make available additional support for special schools, pupils and students with special needs within mainstream schools and FE, those being educated in hospital and teachers of learners with special needs.
>
> (DfEE, 1997a)

Government policy focuses on the need for increasing inclusion of pupils with special educational needs in mainstream schools and to create a situation where parents have real choice of a mainstream placement. Special schools are still seen as vital in providing advice, support and expertise to assist in this transition and will play a key role in the development of an inclusive system. The Green Papers *Excellence for all Children* (DfEE 1997b) and *Meeting Special Educational Needs* (DfEE 1998) set out a framework for that vision and a map of how it might be achieved. The vision recognised that local authorities, possibly working in regional partnerships, should provide the strategic management to ensure all learners' needs are met but schools should receive most of the funding and responsibility for ensuring those needs are met.

Excellence for all Children set an objective that by 2002:

> there will be more effective and widespread use of Information and Communications Technology to support the education of children with SEN, in both mainstream and special schools . . .

> Our policies for raising standards are for *all* children, including those with SEN. Early identification of difficulties and appropriate intervention will give children with SEN the best possible start to their school lives. Our initiatives for improving literacy and numeracy, introducing target setting for schools and opening up

new technologies will help children with SEN reach their full potential.

(DfEE 1997b: 11)

The SEN Code of Practice (DfES 2001a) and the Special Educational Needs and Disability Act (DfES 2001b), with their associated guidance, lay out the legal requirement and also provide advice on how schools and teachers should ensure that pupils' special needs are met. The passing of the Special Educational Needs and Disability Act in 2001 required mainstream schools to put in place policies and strategies to ensure that pupils with disabilities could be readily and fully included within the environment of their school. Funding to make school environments more accessible was made available through the School Access Initiative. The SEN and Disability Act requires schools to make reasonable accommodation to ensure that pupils with disabilities are not discriminated against and are provided with access to the same curriculum as their peers. ICT is an obvious tool to ensure that happens and examples of practice are being developed for publication by DfES and BECTA.

As the National Grid has developed there have been a number of initiatives directed at or important in the field of SEN. The *Modernising Government* White Paper (Cabinet Office 1999), proposed that 50 per cent of all government services to the citizen and to business should be available on-line by 2005 and 100 per cent by 2008, with communication with schools largely by electronic means by 2002. During 1998–2001 there was a proliferation of education sites in the UK commercial, voluntary sector and government. The National Grid for Learning, the UK education portal, by 2001 hosted over 300,000 pages. These developments were significant in a number of ways:

- Previously, paper-based information came into schools and did not necessarily get to the person who needed it: using ICT, anyone with Internet access can get to the information they wanted.
- Getting up-to-date, relevant information to people who need it is easier but care needs to be taken not to overwhelm teachers with a large volume of material.
- There is direct support for classroom activities delivered in an interactive way.

Information on the World Wide Web

The modern teacher supporting pupils with special needs has a wide range of information needs. Communications technology can provide an effective way of meeting many of them. The Internet already has the ability to provide access to information and advice and curriculum planning ideas as well as on-line learning activities. Currently there is an abundance of information.

A simple search on the Internet for a particular area of special needs, such as autism, could easily result in half a million documents and resources being returned. This has its problems in terms of searching and sorting relevant information. An alternative would be to look for sites that you know of and identify specific information in that organisation's site. You could, for example, go to the DfES SEN area knowing you would find policy guidance and other official information. The QCA site provides information on entitlement and curriculum access, and the TTA site details of training, continuous professional development (CPD) and research. Another solution, provided by an increasing number of Internet sites, is to use a portal that allows you to link to a whole range of information that you want, when you want it, which has already been put under convenient headings. Increasingly, LEAs provide this type of service to their schools and include links to recommended external sites which have SEN information or curriculum content.

In 2000 BECTA, working with the DfEE, developed a site which points to a range of dispersed resource information in a quick and easy way and ensures the content is UK-specific and of educational relevance. As part of the National Grid for Learning a Web site called Inclusion provides a catalogue of resources. Designed to help teachers, parents and others involved in meeting pupils' individual needs, this site enables people with information on SEN and inclusion on the Internet to publish that information on the Inclusion site. The search mechanism on the site allows users to find relevant resources by selecting a number of key words from menus. This site also provides a 'Key documents' area giving quick access to legislation and guidance from government departments and agencies in the area of inclusion and special needs.

Inclusion and other sites, such as TeacherNet and the Teacher Resource Exchange, can save teachers time in locating resources and, thanks to the quality assurance process, give them confidence that the resources found are educationally relevant.

Discussion groups

The ability to communicate with peers and others, to exchange ideas, seek help and clarify understanding, is also central to helping teachers do their work effectively. Through the NGfL there are a growing number of mailing lists and Web forums that enable high-quality professional discussion to take place in an electronic form. In 2001 there were about twenty lists focusing on aspects of special educational needs and inclusion.

In 1996 an e-mail list was set up to support special educational needs co-ordinators (SENCOs) called SENCO Forum. The focus of the list was to provide support for SENCOs' day-to-day work and welcomed membership of those who support SENCOs. By 2001 the number of members had increased to around 1,000 and a significant number regularly sent messages. Like any other community, real or electronic, the membership is constantly changing, with people joining, reading messages, leaving and maybe joining again at another time. Analysis of the messages revealed that communications reflected the day-to-day concerns of SENCOs as well as topical or broader teacher concerns. Communication was mainly about meeting the specific needs of pupils, how to make the curriculum accessible, supporting the management and administrative functions of SENCOs and how to use e-mail and Web technology more efficiently.

The use of SENCO Forum was subject to a number of evaluations during the initial phase and these can be accessed on the BECTA Web site. The reports reflect that SENCOs found this form of electronic communication clearly supported their work. It was always clear that the forum would only supplement SENCOs' other information sources. However, individual SENCOs' access to other sources, such as local courses, SENCO groups, teachers' centres and relevant library materials, varied greatly. The evaluation report showed that the forum helped in a number of ways. Above all, SENCO Forum has helped to overcome the isolation which many SENCOs feel in being placed in the position of an expert in their schools without the necessary professional development and support:

> I have found the support I have received from the Internet community overwhelming, and this has reduced my feeling of isolation . . .
>
> . . . instead of reinventing the wheel, you can draw on others' experience . . .

By providing immediate support:

> more or less instant access to people who have answers to your questions . . .
>
> it was important to gather information relating to [the condition of] one of our pupils quickly . . . As a result of the enquiry . . . [the information gathered] was offered to the parents within a matter of hours.

By offering valid and up-to-date advice, because it comes from those:

> who understand the realities of working within the limitations of school systems, classrooms etc.

By giving access to information sources beyond local resources:

> it provides . . . a wealth of experience at an almost instant and national . . . scale from other interested users discussion that gives a fresh angle on issues.

And by fitting in with personal constraints on time:

> being able to communicate with people who aren't always in the office . . .
>
> I can send a request for information down the line, instead of waiting until the support teacher comes next week.
>
> (Wedell 1997: 13–14)

The success of this particular means of communication resulted in a whole range of new lists being created for different communities of teachers and other education professionals. These reflected particular areas of disability or learning difficulty or in some cases teachers' roles. Further details of the range of inclusion and SEN lists available can be found on the BECTA Web site. Increasingly, integration of Web-based forums and e-mail can provide a wider range of facilities for teachers to communicate effectively. This is likely to develop further as teachers in training gain confidence and competence to use a range of electronic mediums. Other tools have been developed centrally to help teachers of pupils with special educational needs. These include the Teacher Resource Exchange, which enables teachers to develop and share ideas for activities and resources electronically, using an on-line database.

The future

So how far have we achieved the aspirations put forward in those Green Papers at the end of the last century? How much closer are we to achieving an inclusive education system where all teachers use ICT confidently and competently to support all students? What will happen next and how far do we still need to travel?

Targets for having all schools connected to the Internet by 2002 look likely to be met, but for many schools, particularly primary schools, it may be a single Internet-connected computer. When sufficient high-speed Internet access can be delivered to schools, giving the opportunity for every student to use the Internet as required, the vision of ICT being as ubiquitous as electricity will be realised. The indications are that NOF training in the use of ICT for teachers and school librarians will meet its target of training all those teachers who need it. However, this represents only a baseline of competence and as new technologies develop teachers will need to keep abreast of them.

The NGfL has developed significantly but lacks the full range of curriculum content and a mechanism for teachers to locate individual resources with precision. Funding for Curriculum Online (2001) and developments in the use of meta-data (key words) and more sophisticated search engines look likely to address these concerns. In 2001 the rights of parents of pupils with special educational needs and disabilities were strengthened by primary legislation and a new SEN Code of Practice. This has the potential to reduce the administrative burden of SENCOs and schools and establish consistency of practice. Regional partnerships of local education authorities in strategic management of special needs have been created, and the pooling of expertise and resources looks likely to benefit pupils.

The National Curriculum (QCA 1999) incorporated a comprehensive Inclusion Statement which more fully described a pupil's curriculum entitlement and indicated where ICT may be of benefit. OFSTED also provided further guidance, *Evaluating Educational Inclusion* (2000) which ensures that inspections continue to look at special needs provision in schools and also address broader inclusion issues.

At the time of writing the government was setting out its agenda for 2001–05 and considering how best to move the whole NGfL initiative forward. It was consulting on how to support teachers' on-going professional development needs in the use of ICT. Issues of sustainable investment in ICT and real costs of ownership were also being explored. There was recognition that there is a need for high-speed Internet connections in all schools to provide access to interactive multimedia learning resources. The need to find the best way of funding the development of resources is explored in *Curriculum On-line* (DfEE 2001a). There are still a number of areas where we need to pay close attention to ensure that the National Grid for Learning provides a service for all learners. Government has been increasingly aware of the importance of creating Web sites that are accessible to learners with disabilities. However, sites and resources that form part of the NGfL more broadly also need to adopt those protocols. *Curriculum Online* must ensure that digital learning resources are appropriate to the whole range of pupils' abilities and do not exclude the most able or those with complex needs. Proposed developments, from government, such as the Cybrarian, an easy way for pupils and other to locate appropriate content on the Internet by using facilities such as speech input, could advantage many pupils, including some with special educational needs.

> The intention is that the Cybrarian will be available through the Web on digital TV, computers and at UK on-line centres, libraries and schools. It will use voice recognition to allow people to 'ask' the Cybrarian about a particular topic, which will guide them to relevant materials. It should . . . particularly help new computer users, those with poor information handling skills, poor literacy skills or visual impairment and those with English as an additional language (EAL).
>
> (DfEE 2001b)

Countries such as Finland are exploring the possibility of creating a symbol-based interface with their national grid. A similar development could usefully be encouraged in the UK. Critical to its success, however, would be ensuring that appropriate resources underlie the portal, and these may need to be pump-primed. The brave new world of an ICT-rich educational community, sharing information, ideas and resources using technology is developing. Teachers of pupils with SEN and the pupils themselves are all benefiting – indeed, in some areas they are leading the field. But more still needs to be done and the journey has not always been easy. Getting to grips with what are sometimes complex technologies and applying them in a range of educational contexts has been made even more daunting by the range of initiatives schools have to implement.

Nevertheless, as we move along the road a point will come when technology is seen not as yet another challenge but a tool to tame and implement the many challenges teachers have to face. It will provide support, spread ideas and good practice, enable the administrative work of schools to be automated to a large degree and break down the isolation which so often leads to the time-consuming reinvention of wheels. In 1997 Dennis Stevenson said:

> We wish to see a society within ten years where ICT has permeated the entirety of education (as it will the rest of society) so that it is no longer a talking point but taken for granted.
>
> (Stevenson 1997)

We are not there yet but the vision is beginning to appear on the horizon.

Summary

- There is support available, in terms of policies for and practical provision of ICT tools which, if well managed, can effect real change in schools.
- Between 1998 and 2004 the government will have committed over £1 billion of expenditure to improve schools' ICT facilities.
- In 1999 the New Opportunities Fund set up a four-year programme 'ICT Training for Teachers, School Librarians, and Public Librarians'.
- Government policy focuses on the need for increasing inclusion of pupils with special educational needs in mainstream schools.
- The Internet already has the ability to provide access to information and advice and curriculum planning ideas as well as on-line learning activities.
- The development of the National Grid for Learning portal provides a mechanism for teachers and others to easily locate the best educational resources around.
- Inclusion and other sites, such as TeacherNet and the Teacher Resource Exchange, can save teachers time in locating relevant resources.
- Through the NGfL there are a growing number of mailing lists and Web forums that enable high-quality professional discussion to take place in electronic form.
- The creation of an ICT-rich educational community, sharing information, ideas and resources using technology, is becoming a reality. Teachers of pupils with SEN and the pupils themselves are benefiting.

References

BECTA (2001) *Primary Schools of the Future: Achieving Today. A Report to the DfEE by BECTA*, Coventry: Becta.

Cabinet Office (1999) *White Paper: Modernising Government*, London: Stationery Office.

DfEE (1997a) *Connecting the Learning Society*, London: HMSO.

DfEE (1997b) *Excellence for all Children: Meeting Special Educational Needs*, London: HMSO.

DfEE (1998a) *Meeting Special Educational Needs: A Programme of Action*, London: DfEE.

DfEE (1998b) *Open for Learning, Open for Business*, London: DfEE.

DfEE (2001a) *Curriculum On-line: a consultation paper*, London: DfEE.

DfEE (20001b) Press release 'School Access Initiative', 13 March, reference in *50M for Access in Schools*, London: DfEE.

DfEE (2001c) Press release, 'Cybrarian', 2 April, referred to in *Digital TV and the Internet to help Pupils tackle Pythagoras and boost GCSE Standards*, London: DfEE.

DfEE and QCA (1999) 'Inclusion: providing effective learning opportunities for all pupils' in *The National Curriculum: Handbook for Primary Teachers in England*, London: QCA.

DfES (2001a) *Special Educational Needs: Code of Practice*, London: Stationery Office.

DfES (2001b) *Special Educational Needs and Disability Act 2001*, London: Stationery Office.

NOF (2000) *ICT Training for Teachers and School Librarians: Information for Schools*, London: New Opportunities Fund (NOF), available on-line at www.nof.org.uk/edu/download/pdf/ict_teng.pdf.

OFSTED (2000) *Evaluating Educational Inclusion: Guidance to School Inspectors*, London: OFSTED.

OFSTED (2001a) *ICT in Schools: the Impact of Government Initiatives*, London: OFSTED.

OFSTED (2001b) *Annual Report of HM Chief Inspector of Schools, 1999–2000: Standards and Quality in Education*, London: OFSTED.

QCA (1999) Curriculum Inclusion Statement, UK National Curriculum, www.nc.uk.net/inclusion.html

Stevenson, D. (1997) *Information and Communications Technology in UK Schools: an independent inquiry*, London: Independent ICT in Schools Commission.

TTA (1999) *National Special Educational Needs Specialist Standards*, London: Teacher Training Agency.

Wedell, K. (1997) *SENCOs Sharing Solutions: An Evaluation of the SENCO Electronic Communication Project*, Coventry: NCET.

Web sites

The National Grid for Learning   www.ngfl.gov.uk
Inclusion   inclusion.ngfl.gov.uk
TeacherNet   www.dfes.gov.uk/teachers/
Teacher Resource Exchange   contribute.ngfl.gov.uk/
Senco-forum   www.becta.org.uk/inclusion/discussion/senfor.html
New Opportunities Fund   www.nof.org.uk/index.htm

Chapter 13

Developing an LEA Web site to support the inclusion process

John Galloway

Local education authorities have a role to play in supporting inclusion, as do the national and government agencies. From his perspective as an advisory teacher for ICT and special educational needs (SEN), John Galloway discusses the issues that need to be considered by a local education authority (LEA).

Educational inclusion is a process, the journey rather than the destination. It is therefore difficult to determine when we will be able to say that we have achieved inclusive education. LEAs are charged with guiding their schools along the road, and they will need to provide information, direction and strategic support. This chapter will consider how the activities of an LEA in developing inclusive education can be supported by use of the Internet.

An LEA will ensure that the principles of educational inclusion inform all its activities; that educational opportunities are open to all pupils regardless of their social or ethnic background or any particular special educational needs. There is an argument that if this is the case there is no need for an inclusive education Web site, as the philosophy permeates all of an LEA site's content. However, there are issues pertinent to inclusion that will need to be separately and singularly considered. In this chapter I will discuss the ways in which inclusion will inform all aspects of an LEA Web site as well as considering those which will need particular, individual attention.

What are LEAs doing to develop inclusion?

LEAs are determining the strategic planning and the necessary action to make inclusive education a reality. They are promoting the values, planning the process and taking action. This process is an inclusive one. To be successful it needs to be supported not only by schools but by all the education stakeholders locally. This group includes the immediate school community, staff, pupils and governors, and the wider one of parents, other agencies, community groups and local businesses. The principles of inclusion will underpin all the policies and planning addressing an LEA's activities, not just inclusion or SEN action plans. From the Education Development Plan, through the Behaviour Support Plan, the plans for early years and lifelong learning, to the Professional Development offer, inclusive principles will be evident.

The LEA will lead on promoting the values and ethos necessary to bring about inclusive schools. To do this will require activities to promote the principles, training to put these into action and the building of systems and structures to make them a reality. It will be necessary to ensure that stakeholders have a clear understanding of what is meant by inclusion and of how it will be achieved. All staff, from LEA officers to teachers, teaching assistants, lunchtime supervisors and school keepers will need to develop their skills in order to work with a broad range of children.

Good practice will need to be disseminated and achievements celebrated. Those involved in this process also need support, from experts and from each other. There will need to be access to advice, resources and other people. Different ways of working are happening and new relationships being made.

What is the purpose of an Inclusive Education Web site?

The LEA will need to advertise, to inform and to involve. Its constituents need to know what it is doing, what its principles and goals are, and what is expected of them. A Web site gives an immediately accessible medium for this, as it offers a dynamic means of communication. Content can be multi-layered, easily updated and constantly evolving. New areas can be developed as the process continues, and information can be easily published, amended, updated and readily found. The LEA can advertise its activities, its supporting resources and links with other organisations.

The Internet can inform, as leaflets, articles, letters and notices can, but it can also be dynamic. It can put people in touch with each other and can offer support and resources focused on the task from a single, electronic, source. There is also an opportunity to create networks, dynamic links between people within its area. This can include teacher-to-teacher – the SENCO noticeboard provided by Birmingham at www.bgfl.org in the Staff area, for instance – parents and supporting organisations, access to advice and even pupil-to-pupil. One paradox of inclusion in mainstream schools is that pupils can sometimes feel isolated, and that they are the only one with a particular special need. The Internet can link them up with peers in similar situations. One site, www.adders.org/chat.htm, offers a chat room for people with attention deficit disorder (ADD). This is aimed at people over 16 with guidance notes for users specifying this. There are also sites written from a personal perspective which offer insights into particular conditions. 'Oops wrong planet syndrome' at www.isn.net/~jypsy offers first-hand accounts of autism. (This is also a very rich resource, including over 800 links to other sites.)

A Web site can be a place for celebration, for sharing good practice and for recognising achievement. The dynamic nature of the Internet makes this quickly and easily manageable. Activities that support the process can be shared with not just the local community but potentially the world. Pages can be given over to good practice. Schools trialling particular approaches or resources can offer brief reports. Parent support groups can give updates. Groups of pupils can contribute views. The Sheffield SEN Strategy Consultation Forum publishes strategies and seeks discussion and responses. The forum is:

> a Web-based forum for those with an interest to debate the issues . . . [It] is one strand of our approach to facilitating stakeholders contributing their views to the process.
> (www.steps.org.uk/forum.html#target3, accessed 26 June 2001)

Some schools are individually developing expertise in specific skills. By working with a speech and language team they may be developing their ability to identify problems early on and provide effective interventions throughout a pupil's school career. Whilst not all schools can do this to the same degree, by advertising this initiative they can become a resource for all local schools. The East Sussex Behaviour Support Team offers resources developed in local schools (www.eastsussexcc.gov.uk/edu/inclusion/materials.htm). There is, for instance, a detailed Anger Management Programme which gives the theory of the approach along with downloadable resources to implement it.

How do you go about creating a Web site?

The Internet continues to grow exponentially, but much of the content is of dubious value. The Web space and the software to build a site are readily available. Many Internet service providers give free space and free software, such as Front Page Express, is available to create a minimal presence.

However, the do-it-yourself route is not one that should be readily taken by a corporate entity which will be revealing itself to the world. Professional values will need to be promoted and therefore a professional approach is necessary. Unless professional expertise is readily available in the authority it should be brought in. This may raise management issues, as a degree of control may be lost. It will be necessary to write a clear brief, even detailing the number of pages to be created. Corporate identity will need to be maintained throughout. Pages will need to conform to a house style, to be navigable in the same way, and to use uniform logos and buttons. ICT projects notoriously always overrun, both in time and money. The end result may not work quite as intended and the menus may become misnomers – content not found where the user might expect it to be. Navigation may become flawed and links to other sites can become redundant as these develop or close. It is therefore important to build in flexibility and to tightly manage the posting of content.

There is also the possibility of creating an intranet. This is a private area, often run over a network rather than the Web, where confidential information can be posted. It is possible to create a virtual intranet by having password-protected areas on a Web site. This allows access from an Internet connection, thereby precluding the need for users to be on a single network.

When building a site useful guidance on ensuring that it is accessible can be found at the Centre for Applied Special Technology (CAST) site. Apart from guidance on building accessible Web sites there is also a tool, Bobby, which will automatically check any Web page against accessibility guidelines (www.cast.org/bobby). The Plain English Campaign also offers guidance on building accessible Web sites at www.plainenglish. co.uk/Web siteguide.html.

What should go on the site?

In the first instance the intention is clearly to inform. The site is a means to convey information quickly to others. All the authority's information relating to inclusion can be called up from a single source. Anything that is published on paper can be published electronically, although some would be better placed on the Internet and others on an intranet. Several LEAs publish relevant policies on their Web sites. Bristol (www.bristol-lea.org.uk/teaching/sen/frameworks.html) has a page with relevant policies including such things as SEN, manual handling of children and home-to-school transport. Other authorities have published their Inclusive Education Development Plan – see, for instance, Tower Hamlets at www.towerhamlets-pdc.org.uk/policies.php?id=5&type=50.

The information will be as varied as the audience. This will include teachers, governors, parents, other professionals – locally, nationally and, potentially, globally. Content could include anything that would ordinarily enter the public domain, such as press releases and consultation documents, as well as content written specifically for the site, such as local action plans.

In the first category are:

- strategic plans;
- statistics;
- guidance to professionals and parents;
- information and contact details about local support teams;
- teaching resources;
- links to other sites;
- news;
- summaries of government and LEA documents.

Local content can include:

- the training offer;
- training materials;
- details of support groups;
- information about initiatives and projects;
- local news;
- summaries of conferences;
- information about schools with expertise or additional resourcing for specific needs such as hearing impairment.

By developing an intranet it is possible to circulate the kind of information that would normally go out in the internal mail, but much more immediately and quickly, with the possibility of rapid responses. This might include:

- requests for information;
- invitations to join working parties;
- organisational changes;
- information about available grants;
- internal documentation such as requests for assessment and support.

A closed area also allows for the development of support mechanisms. Notice boards or bulletin boards can put people in touch with each other. This process creates both an inclusive community and a dynamic site.

What content is exclusively inclusive?

Whilst all content providers on an LEA site will take inclusion into account as a matter of course there will be content that needs to be specifically constructed and posted. A programme of professional development will have references to inclusion throughout, from literacy, numeracy and early years teams, for instance. There may also be particular training, perhaps in the identification of SEN, that may be found only in an inclusive education area. Likewise it may be desirable to provide links to other training providers working in particular fields, such as the National Autistic Society (www.oneworld.org/autism_uk/courses/confer.html).

There may be particular resources an LEA can offer. Tower Hamlets has an IEP template with a Microsoft Word AutoText target bank (www.towerhamlets-pdc.org.uk/resources.php?id=5&type=10). Or links can be offered to national resources like the DfES guidance on identifying dyslexia in the classroom (www.dfee.gov.uk/sen/hints.htm). Sheffield has a variety of resources that can be downloaded at www.steps.org.uk/resourcemenu.html.

Professional development goes beyond training. Expertise is also developed through reading about research and the experience of others. Links to articles and expertise internationally such as those at the Office for Special Education at the University of Virginia (aace.virginia.edu/curry/dept/cise/ose/home.html) enable this process. BECTA offers a range of professional groups, including SENIT and the SENCO Forum. Found at www.becta.org.uk/inclusion/discussion/bectalists.html, these put practitioners directly in touch with each other, raising questions and eliciting responses. A question or issue can be raised and quickly responded to by others who have had similar experiences or concerns.

An intranet can also offer such dynamic interactivity at a local level. One important aspect of developing inclusive education locally is to draw upon local experience. Staff working with pupils with low incidence needs can, through bulletin boards or newsgroups, seek support from others within the LEA without the need to meet, as has happened in Birmingham. Teachers may be more comfortable communicating with others in the same locality than with those in national or international groups. Locality can be important when issues of incidence, resourcing and support are discussed. In an individual school teachers may feel that they are working in isolation: across an LEA they can link to others who are addressing similar problems and enter into a dialogue with them.

In one authority there may be only a comparatively small number of pupils with Down's syndrome, for instance: some in mainstream classrooms and some in special schools. By giving the opportunity for practitioners to communicate, at a time that is convenient to them, a working dialogue can be developed. Local information about support and resourcing can be shared, and ways of working quickly checked and reinforced.

One area that may need careful consideration is the management of news. National content, such as DfES activities, can be brought in or linked to. However, the Internet offers the opportunity to publish local news instantly. This could be a school's practice in a particular area such as teaching PE to physically impaired pupils. Appropriate extracts from OFSTED reports can celebrate good practice. It could be the work of a particular group of teachers, developing reporting mechanisms, or pupils' achievements, or activities of a community group. Some schools such as Meldreth Manor (www.meldrethmanor.com) or Ambleside Primary School (www.ambleside.schoolzone.co.uk/ambleweb/classwk. htm) have sites that are designed to share pupils' work and to celebrate achievements. This could be developed at an LEA Web site level, following particular collaborative initiatives, for instance. A group of teaching assistants completing a City and Guilds or Key Skills course may not hit the headlines elsewhere but can be recognised on an LEA site. This may encourage others within the authority to take the course, and other education authorities to implement it.

Keeping up to date with news within the LEA means having mechanisms either to seek it out or that feed it into the site. It is sometimes easy to become focused on a handful of high-profile schools and miss what is happening elsewhere. Reporting structures, from the advisory team or educational psychologists for instance, can broaden the site's content by gathering in information. Schools that may ordinarily be shy can have their achievements acknowledged too.

Up-to-date news will help to build traffic as people visit the site to find out what is happening. By creating mechanisms such as putting the site on the agenda of all team meetings news can be gathered and posted quickly. Schools and teachers seeing the site as a source of news will, in turn, offer articles to be posted.

In building an LEA Web site what issues need to be considered?

There are a number of issues to be resolved when developing a site, not least of which is that of ownership. Is it entirely a tool of LEA administration and management or does it serve a wider purpose, to build a supportive community of education stakeholders? Or can it be both?

As a vehicle for the authority's administrative and management functions the Internet has many strengths. All the information the LEA wants to give out can be easily and immediately made available. For users this offers one place to go to find information, resources and links to other sites. However, it may also mean that users view it as a one-way street; information is given but not received. Another route is to bring potential users together, such as SENCOs, specialist teachers, educational psychologists, managers and governors, and ask them to determine the content and structure that they will find useful. The Sheffield STEPS site (Support Teaching and Education Psychology Service, www.steps. org.uk) brings the work of these teams together.

These two approaches may produce similar results, or they may not. From an LEA perspective this raises the issue of editorial control. If the site is badged as the education authority's then content must reflect policy and priorities. In many instances this will be the case. However, teachers at the chalk-face may sometimes have a different perspective from that of officers and members. One example of such dissonance is in the posting of exemplar Inclusive Education Policies. It is often helpful for schools to have policy document templates drafted that can be adapted to the local context, and this is not uncommon in curriculum areas. Tower Hamlets publishes an outline ICT policy. However, when formulating policy on inclusion this may be too prescriptive, offering a correct model of inclusion rather than expecting schools to determine its nature in their own circumstances.

It is likely that a users' group would want such support with developing policy. Schools could post their own documents, thereby offering others guidance and the possibility of debate and discussion. However, if this were done through the LEA a number of issues would arise. First it would imply endorsement by the authority of an approved approach. Secondly it may encourage schools to develop only in the ways advertised. Finally such policies may need to change as the inclusion process moves on.

There is the possibility of a collaborative model: the site is owned by the LEA but with parts of it being given over to a user group to populate. Whilst this approach adds an administrative task, of holding meetings, even virtual ones, and acting on outcomes, it will mean that the site's content is directly addressed by the needs of practitioners. Ownership becomes shared, as is the process of inclusion.

What systems and structures will be necessary to manage the site?

Most Web sites with a large amount of content have a Web master (or mistress) to look after them. This is often someone with advanced IT skills capable of dealing with the technical issues. However, technical issues may be quite low on the list of needs for managing the site in order to meet the LEA's objectives.

If, as has been suggested, the inclusion content of a Web site is intended to inform and to involve then the key management issue is how to bring this about. How does the content get gathered, posted, refreshed and reviewed? It is preferable to see the Web master/mistress as an information manager who posts content and builds systems that support the site's development and sustenance. It is possible to manage a site without advanced knowledge of HTML authoring if the site is structured for this. The content is more important than the technical details.

There are a number of ways of bringing in content. One is to make it policy to write everything for the Web with paper copies being a spin-off. This is not difficult to do. Almost all software produced in recent years gives the option of saving in HTML format. Programs such as Microsoft Publisher will allow you to publish to the Web and provides a Design Checker to facilitate this. Powerpoint presentations can be easily converted. Microsoft Word saves immediately as HTML or can be copied and pasted into database-style sites.

It is necessary to ensure that staff are thinking about the Internet as a medium of communication. By making it a standing item on all agendas, even one that seldom gets a response, staff will be prompted to think about its use and begin to explore the possibilities. One issue will be editorial control of content. How is it determined that the content reflects policy? There are at least two possibilities. One is to produce an editorial content policy document; another is to introduce structures whereby everything posted is authorised by a senior manager. A combination of the two will allow sufficient autonomy for the site manager to post information whilst being clear about when to refer up.

Such a policy will refer to the needs of the intended audience; publishing content already in the public domain; key policy objectives that should be considered when publishing; legal requirements; the style of content; content that is inappropriate, and systems and structures for validating and authorising content that is not covered by other elements. There may already be in existence guidance, such as that for press releases, that covers some or all of these areas. Guidance on content is less manageable if dynamic areas such as bulletin boards are created. The nature of these areas is to allow peer-to-peer contact. LEA contributions may be welcome, by question-and-answer sessions with education psychologists or advisers, for example, but if tightly controlled these areas can become sterile and unused. There is a balance to be struck between using the site as a tool of management and administration and using it to create a dynamic, supportive community.

Why should anybody visit the site?

Effectively this is the starting point. If there is no good reason to visit the site there is no good reason to create it. Here are a few of the possible reasons. There will be more.

- They find it supports their practice.
- They can find the answers to their questions.
- They can easily access help and guidance.
- It allows them to feel included.
- They can find documentation and resources in one place.
- It puts them in touch with the LEA – its thinking and activities.
- It keeps them up to date.

However, unless the site is promoted and monitored it may not receive the desired response. Once created, the site needs to be promoted as a tool for supporting inclusion. School staff need to be made aware of its content and the reasons why they might want to go there. Parents, community groups and other stakeholders will need to know about this resource and what it can offer them.

Once promoted, it is possible to monitor the traffic on the site. Statistics may be available from the host of the Web site on which pages are receiving hits and the sources of those hits (not the individual but their Internet service provider). This will give rough guidance as to whether local schools and the community are accessing the site and to what degree there is interest from elsewhere.

Summary

- An Inclusive Education Web site can promote and support the activities of an LEA.

- It can be a valuable tool in moving forward along the road to inclusive education.

- It is a powerful instrument for communicating, advertising and disseminating.

- An LEA Web site offers its own particular, dynamic means of moving the process on.

Chapter 14

Inclusion through ICT
The wider view

Anne Phelan

Much has been said about the use of the Internet in special needs education. However, questions arise as to the penetration of Internet use in this field outside a small number of schools and innovators and the actions that might be taken to support more widespread Internet use. This chapter sets information and communication technology (ICT) and the Internet in the context of special needs education policy and practice internationally, indicates the Irish situation via case studies and statistics, outlines major barriers to Internet use in special needs and finally suggests factors to be considered and action to be taken to spread Internet use beyond the bounds of the minority to the majority.

Context: international policy and practice

In the 1990s many Western countries launched three or four-year programmes to introduce, or better integrate, ICT into schools. Although many policies reference special needs and the advantages of using ICT with special needs students, few include specific policy objectives or implementation strategies to support ICT in special needs education in general, and Internet use in special education in particular. In fact the European Agency for Development in Special Needs Education surveyed the ICT and special educational needs (SEN) policy and practice in its eighteen member countries in 2000 and found that none of the respondent countries had an ICT and SEN-specific policy. The European Agency for Development in Special Needs Education is an independent, self-governing organisation supported by the Ministries of Education of its fifteen member states and the European Commission. Details of the survey responses are found under the individual country names on its Web site. None of the respondent countries had an SEN and ICT-specific policy as at 1 July 2001 (www.european-agency.org/ict_sen_db/).

The Irish government launched a three-year national project to integrate technology into teaching and learning in schools between 1998 and 2000 with many specific targets. These targets were intended to be applicable to all teachers and students; none of them specifically referenced special needs (Irish Department of Education and Science 1997). Other national plans note some specific advantages in using ICT with SEN students and that targeted measures may be needed, but again do not specify how to ensure that SEN students gain these advantages or identify what targeted measures are needed (e.g. Danish Ministry of Education 1998; Education Network Australia 2000). A notable European exception to this trend is Sweden; its national ICT in schools programme set significant action concerning the use of ICT in special education (Swedish Ministry of Education and Science 1998).

One of the results of no specific policy on ICT and SEN is that there is often no systematic monitoring or evaluation of ICT in SEN policy implementation. Given that this is the case with ICT in special education in general, it is clear that policies and implementation plans to support and promote the Internet and special education also tend to be somewhat underdeveloped. That said, a number of countries are now taking specific action to promote the Internet in education, e.g. Belgium and the Netherlands. Again it is noteworthy that few such actions are specifically directed at special education, although some may be tailored to include special education requirements.

Although the Internet was not originally designed as a resource for education, teachers are identifying key roles for the Internet in education. These include:

- professional development, both informal (through access to information, communication, resources) and formal (through distance learning);
- support and communication, through networking and access to remote services;
- access to and publishing of information and curriculum resources, such as lesson plans for class preparation;
- classroom use, including information gathering, Web publishing, projects and communication (e-mail, etc.).

In Sweden 'there are more than ten specially designed Web sites to support teachers working in special education. . . . These also act as networks to support teachers in their use of ICT with students with SENs'. There is more information about Sweden on the agency's Web site, as there is regarding all the national responses. National and global sharing of resources and information features strongly in Norway's plans. In Portugal the central issues include the provision of distance and local support through networks as well as through resource and information centres. Some special schools in Greece already share their software via the Internet, demonstrating another potential use and the value of the Internet to countries which do not always have an obvious use for the English language-dominated Internet.

The Internet and SEN in Ireland: case studies, lesson learnt and statistics

In Ireland one of the specific actions taken to promote the use of ICT involved supporting innovative projects. The main route for such support has been channelled through the Schools Integration Project (SIP) initiative, implemented by the National Centre for Technology in Education (NCTE), which encompassed over eighty school-based ICT projects. More information about these projects can be found on the NCTE's Web site (www.ncte.ie) and through in published form (NCTE 2000).

Such projects often lead the way in Internet use and expand the boundaries of teachers', and indeed policy makers', thinking on the role of the Internet in special education. Some examples of innovative ICT projects in Ireland follow.

SIP: using video-conferencing to support an incapacitated student

This project demonstrated the use of video-conferencing as a tool of inclusion through distance communication. The project, based in Sligo, enabled students confined to home for whatever reason, be it illness, disability or pregnancy, to participate in their regular classes through video-conferencing between home and school. The student saw and heard her class on the computer and asked, or was asked, questions like any other student. This system allows participating students to keep up to date with their school and homework and to keep in contact with their peers and teachers. Direct-dial ISDN was used between the student's home and the school. More information about this project can be found on the NCTE Web site in the Special Needs section.

SIP: Startech

The Startech project also demonstrated how otherwise isolated teachers and students can receive services, communicate and co-operate at a distance using video-conferencing. Some students living on an island off the coast were in need of a learning support (remedial) service on a regular basis. Weather conditions, however, do not always permit journeys to and from the island. A video-conferencing facility enabled lessons to be delivered by the learning support teacher, based on the mainland, to students in the island school. The Technical category of the NCTE Web site has more details of the project. The mainstream teachers also used the system to consult the learning support teacher on the students' progress, thereby reducing their isolation as well as that of the students. This link is just one example of a number of video-conferencing links made possible by the Startech project for different educational purposes.

SIP: Sun Microsystems pilot project

Moving to students with learning disabilities, very few projects in Ireland have investigated the use of the Internet with these students in any structured fashion. The Sun Microsystems pilot project investigated the integration of the Internet into the curriculum, the networking/sharing of teaching resources through the Net and its use as a publishing medium for students. It involves a number of schools, including the St John of God special school (homepage.eircom.net/~johnofgodschool) which caters mainly for children with moderate general learning disabilities. The special school initially concentrated its efforts on researching Internet use, training teachers and integrating technology into the teaching of communication, language and literacy. Teachers received training in the creation of individualised learning materials and a Web site has been designed and produced as part of the project which includes the work of many classes for publication on the site.

Cyber Campus

The Cyber Campus project (www.internet-ireland.ie/horizon) demonstrates how the Internet can be used in a distance learning programme. Run by the Cystic Fibrosis Association of Ireland, it caters for students who are confined to home by illness. In operation since 1996, the project provides vocational training in IT skills for older students and young adults through its Web site. A key feature of the course methodology is on-line tutoring, which is delivered to students in real time through an on-line chat facility. In addition, students use e-mail and undertake self-tuition using course materials in hard and soft copy. Like many successful distance learning projects, the additional presence of a face-to-face tutor, who in this case calls to the students' homes once a week, is an essential part of the formula. Since early 2001 the project has broadened its educational brief to include the development of educational content in other areas to be provided through its own Web site and links with other educational Web sites such as ScoilNet.

ScoilNet

The major Irish national undertaking involving the Internet and education to date has been the development of ScoilNet. ScoilNet (www.scoilnet.ie) is a national Web portal developed by the NCTE on behalf of the Irish government's Department of Education and Science, the first phase of which was in partnership with Intel. The site hosts curriculum and other educational resources, and provides facilities for feedback and interaction. Users categorise themselves as a teacher, student or parent on entry to the site, and thereafter can find relevant resources. A special education section has been developed for teachers, much of which is also relevant to, and accessible by, parents. This section contains information, educational resources, advice sheets and links, with the emphasis on providing basic information in a simple structure rather than a large quantity of information. It also utilises a threaded discussion board facility to provide discussion groups related to different types of disabilities.

Issues arising and lessons learnt

The development and implementation of these projects has been an important learning experience for Irish educators. A national evaluation of the Schools Integration Project is to be conducted and will elaborate on issues related to carrying out innovative projects on ICT in schools. Specifically in relation to special education, it is clear from these projects that the potential of a small amount of technology to make a vast improvement in the educational service being delivered to students with special needs has been demonstrated.

The potential of the Internet as a communication and (two-way) transmission tool has been explored through projects using video-conferencing and Internet chat facilities. The video-conferencing projects described above use direct-dial ISDN lines but, as bandwidth increases and quality of the Web-based video-conferencing improves, it will become easier to trial such projects using the Internet. Video-conferencing requires considerable co-operation between the sites to be connected. In the case of home-based students, the co-operation and support of the family are essential. Equally, not every student will adapt or respond to the technology with equal ease and therefore it is difficult to generalise and apply some of the results of these projects to other students and situations. However, the reaction of most teachers involved is that the students adapt more easily than they expect and that participation in the projects has enhanced both the students' educational progress and their self-esteem.

A comprehensive evaluation report of the Cyber Campus project was completed following the initial run of the project (1996–97), which showed that responses to the course and its methodology were very positive (MacMahon 1998). The response rate for the evaluation questionnaire was 75 per cent, and 100 per cent of the students who responded said that they would be interested in doing another training course using computer-based learning and the Internet.

The Sun Microsystems pilot project started slowly, owing to some practical implementation difficulties, but this unforeseen delay meant that the project had the chance to develop a solid base through the phased introduction of ICT, starting with research, then training, then curriculum integration.

Regarding ScoilNet, some complex issues and implementation problems have emerged regarding the integration of special education content and facilities into a Web portal designed for the entire (first and second level) teaching community in Ireland. Some issues that have arisen are:

- the priority to be given to special education within a site which caters for all aspects of education;
- the quality and curriculum relevance of the content, especially given that the special education curriculum is somewhat loosely defined at present;
- the categorisation of resources, information and interactive facilities for easy location, particularly when they are relevant to both mainstream and special education.

As well as content for teachers and parents, it is the NCTE's intention to facilitate the development of special education resources and facilities to be accessed directly by students. However, development of this section has been postponed as a number of additional issues arose which require further exploration, including:

- the need for content intended for direct student access;
- its development (by whom and what content);
- the categorisation or labelling of the content for easy location by the student whilst concurrently avoiding any unwelcome labels;
- its status in relation to mainstream content;
- how its design could blend cohesively with the rest of the content in the section (i.e. content directed at mainstream students of a similar age, but not necessarily of similar ability or following the same curriculum).

New curriculum guidelines are being developed for students with general learning disabilities and it is expected that some progress on this section may be made subsequently (NCCA 1999). An update on developments is available at www.ncca.ie.

While these projects have taught us valuable lessons, more work needs to be done in identifying how best to use the Internet for specific target groups, particularly in the education of students with general learning disabilities.

The statistical picture in Irish special schools

The above innovative projects represent the more innovative schools in terms of ICT integration. But what of the general picture? Statistical information supports the experience of the NCTE that, while Irish special needs teachers are making considerable efforts to include the Internet in their teaching, they are clearly experiencing some difficulty in doing so, perhaps owing in part to some of the barriers noted below. Statistics on Internet connectivity and use in special schools were gathered prior to and post the implementation of its three-year Schools IT2000 project in a survey of all schools. The statistics were collected under the auspices of NCTE and compiled in unpublished reports by Aidan Mulkeen and his research team at the National University of Ireland, Maynooth.

These statistics show fairly widespread, if limited, Internet use in a special school context. The percentage of teacher use of the Internet in special schools was higher than that of student use, the main use being for research purposes. Twelve per cent of schools provided e-mail accounts for teachers and less than 5 per cent provided such accounts for students. Fifty per cent of schools have an acceptable use policy for Internet safety, but only 12 per cent reported using filtering software to prevent unsuitable material being viewed on the Internet. Fifteen per cent have a Web site, a third of which carry project or curricular work done by students.

In terms of connectivity and bandwidth, one of the first actions of the Schools IT2000 project was to provide an Internet connection for every school. At the commencement of the project in 1998, 25 per cent of primary and special schools had an Internet connection, while at the end of the project in 2000 almost all schools had an Internet connection. Ninety per cent of special schools reported having e-mail facilities and only 8 per cent had Internet access on multiple machines. Twelve per cent of respondents reported having ISDN access, with the remainder connecting to the Internet via an ordinary, PSDN telephone line.

These statistics suggest that special schools in Ireland are at an early stage of development as far as the Internet is concerned in terms of both penetration of connectivity within schools and Internet use. Regarding teacher skills in ICT, 88 per cent of teachers reported having some skill in ICT and 70 per cent reported some skill on the Internet. However, more ICT training for teachers is listed as the top priority for special schools.

With regard to schools' ICT priorities, 'Internet access on more computers' and 'faster Internet access' came quite low on a list of fourteen priorities (ninth and eleventh respectively). Over 40 per cent of schools stated that they were happy with the level of access their school had to the Internet. It is difficult to say why Internet access comes low on the list of priorities, although, to date, teachers and others have used educational software in the curriculum rather than the Internet. Another recent Irish survey found that the ICT priorities of SEN resource teachers also related to software and professional development in their selection, use and integration with the curriculum rather than with the Internet (IATSE 2000: 4).

Using the Internet in class: some barriers

The other chapters and the above case studies have indicated what is possible in terms of Internet use in special needs and there are many books and Web sites with lesson plans and providing practical ideas for using the Internet in education in general, many of which can also be used in special education (e.g. Lamb *et al.* 1998). However, reviews of the literature and the opinions of teachers indicate a long list of other quite specific barriers to using the Internet in special education classes. The key problems relate to making the Internet accessible to students, design issues, the inherent characteristics of the Web and the characteristics of special needs students themselves and how they interact with the Web.

The issue of Internet access for students with physical, sensory and specific learning difficulties is covered in more detail elsewhere in this book. Such students may need to use assistive technology in order to access the Internet, but even when this technology is available, access may be problematic because the content is often not designed for access through such technology (e.g. Web sites designed without screen readers in mind). Access for students with general learning difficulties can also be problematic. Berry (2000: 51) notes that 'Web sites and pages frequently (and unfortunately) are haphazard design attempts which combine a vast number of different and often incomprehensible screen elements in a format which is awkward and difficult to follow'. This results in much cognitive processing effort being devoted to interpreting the page rather than concentrating on its content.

Although accessible design is essential, it is only part of the solution to the problems faced by SEN teachers. The nature of the Web itself poses both advantages and disadvantages to its use; there is a large quantity of uncatalogued and unstable information of different amounts, intended for a wide range of audiences, presented in an inconsistent manner but dominated by textual information. This means that skills in selecting information and in navigating from one piece of information to another will be needed to use it effectively, as will patience with downloading and an understanding of the way the Web is structured. Some of the learning characteristics associated with special needs students may not blend easily with learning through use of the Internet because the aforementioned skills and qualities are not well developed. Berry (2000: 49) notes that 'aspects of the interaction process that occurs between the student and the site may be related to individual differences across students or they may be related to the unique ways in which the student interacts with Web-based materials'. Other learning and behaviour characteristics of special needs students can pose problems, such as difficulty in focusing on the task at hand and impatience, especially with slow Internet downloads. On the other hand, some studies have found that the special needs students in the study focused better on the task at hand through the use of the Internet and learned to cope with the frustrations they encounter in its use (e.g. Goldstein 1998: 17; Smith *et al*. 1998: 26).

Strategies can be applied to help overcome many of the barriers to Internet use with SEN students. 'Sometimes the biggest barriers to Internet access are solved simply by planning ahead and making smart choices about which equipment and software to buy' (Baysha 1998: 4). Baysha's handbook goes on to list a number of issues that arise in special education related to use of the Internet and suggests strategies to adopt in addressing those issues. Having said that, the time, planning and resources it takes to implement these problem-solving strategies effectively should not be underestimated. It is important to recognise that there are a huge range of competing priorities in the special education teacher's day, many of which may be much more important than the use of ICT. Even when the teacher is able to prioritise ICT use, lack of resources may be a significant deterrent to the teacher. In particular, SEN teachers often do not have adequate time or classroom support to design and effectively implement individualised plans for Internet use, especially for those students who need one-to-one assistance.

Moving forward

Much progress has been made in relation to Internet use in SEN although more progress is needed to exploit its capacity fully. But how do we move forward in a realistic way to enable all teachers and schools to use the Internet with their special needs students, to overcome some of the barriers mentioned and to expand on the role of the Internet as an aid to, and medium of, education? The need for legislation to enshrine the rights of students with special needs to the kinds of support and services they need is acutely felt in many countries (US Department of Education 2000), not least in Ireland, where a number of court cases have challenged the government's provision in this area. Legislation can also affect the technology manufacturers and software developers. In the United States legislation has made it impossible for manufacturers and developers to ignore users with disabilities, and some suggest that Europe needs to follow suit (Grogan 2001).

In the absence of legislation there are several other items which can be considered and actions taken at all levels of ICT planning, whether at national policy level or at the level of classroom integration by the teacher. Most of them have been addressed throughout the chapter already; this section draws them together as items to be considered and catered for within any actions being developed to support Internet use in special education. The areas for consideration are:

- policies, plans and procedures;
- professional development;
- educational approach and curriculum;
- resources;
- support and school culture;
- research;
- innovation and its uptake;
- infrastructure.

Policies, plans and procedures

The special education implications of ICT policies, plans and procedures may be forgotten unless there is someone involved in the technology team with a focus on or expertise in this area. Special education content of Internet policy, if it exists at all, may relate solely to access issues, particularly access by visually impaired people, rather than to the range of issues addressed in this chapter. Steering committees of Web sites, editorial groups and technology implementation teams all need a mechanism to ensure that special education is catered for adequately. This idea can be applied at all levels of education, from the teachers implementing ICT plans in their own classes to school-based planning to national policy and planning. The mechanism to be adopted could take a number of forms. Baysha (1998: 11) suggests that special education teacher representation on the school's technology team is a useful mechanism, both to assist with the inclusion of special needs and because his or her input is likely to identify strategies to help technology work better as a learning tool for all students. Another mechanism could be to adopt a procedure whereby all policies, plans and procedures are written down and subjected to a special needs 'check' of some sort, akin to an audit, health check or impact assessment. Such a procedure would ensure that special needs issues are raised. In order to ensure that these issues are also addressed, a policy of inclusion is essential.

Professional development

Professional development is widely recognised as being key to integrating ICT into the curriculum. The experience of the NCTE in 1998–2000 has been that teachers will not use the Internet in school until they have a reasonable degree of access to it and feel comfortable with it themselves. Training is therefore very important, at least in the initial stages of learning Internet skills. However, skill-based training alone is not adequate. In Germany it is increasingly felt that there is a lack of appropriate educational models for applying ICT in this (ICT and SEN) field and therefore a lack of guiding concepts that would come from these models. In this context, more specialist training programmes for teachers are called for everywhere – particularly, as in Germany, training programmes that methodically and didactically focus on ICT in SEN, thus allowing new perspectives in the organisation of teaching using ICT. Teachers themselves are also getting used to new models of professional development as the Internet is increasingly being used for distance learning. This form of learning may particularly suit special education teachers, who need differentiated, specialised training.

Educational approach and curriculum

The above point regarding new perspectives in the organisation of teaching is widely made, with calls for a move away from the traditional didactic method of teaching where the school and teacher are seen as sources of information towards a new paradigm of education in which a constructivist model of education dominates and into which ICT and the Internet fit very well (e.g. Papert 2001). Becker (1999: 28) notes that 'Teachers who regard education as primarily the distribution of facts and skills to students according to a fixed curriculum sequence are much less likely to exploit the Internet than more "constructivist" teachers.' Being realistic, it may take some time for this paradigm shift to happen and professional development in ICT alone will not bring about such a fundamental change.

Changes in the curriculum and educational system will also be needed prior to the widespread adoption of non-traditional educational approaches. At the broadest level, we need to 'look at modern technology with new eyes [and] see computers not as tools with which we can perform old jobs better, but as engines that power completely new tasks' (Thornburg 1996: 97). International trends in special education include differentiated curricula for students with special needs, individual education plans and, in some cases, individual technology plans. Special education has, therefore, great possibilities for adopting a needs-driven educational plan based on a vision which integrates the benefits and uses of technology. Technology, special education and curriculum support/development agencies will need to work together to achieve the integration of technology with special education in general and the curriculum in particular.

At the school level, many school Internet policies concentrate on safety issues rather than on curriculum integration issues. There is a need 'to direct Internet use towards positive curriculum use, to make sure it is used effectively and openly by everyone in the school community' (Grey 1999: 141). In particular there is a need for greater awareness of the uses of the Internet to achieve a lesson outcome, as distinct from using the Internet as a lesson outcome (Franklin 2000: 43).

Resources

Availability of quality accessible educational resources on the Internet, and the ability to manipulate and communicate about these resources, will be essential if the Internet explosion is to reach its full potential in education. A next step in this direction

> will be for publishers of school materials and other companies and organisations that provide materials and services to the schools to try making teaching materials available on the Internet. Such a trend may greatly benefit students who need digital technology to be able to read the material, since it may be their only means of access.
>
> (Gunvall 2000)

It has also been noted in Sweden that there is a need to get a standardised storage format for text, pictures and sounds in teaching materials and software in order to make digital information available, accessible by standardised browsers and capable of being used to meet the needs of the individual. The issue of payment for Internet-based resources will arise once publishers become more active in making their resources available on-line and discussions around the issue of appropriate Internet financial models to grow this market and facilitate access to what it has to offer need to start now.

The term 'resources' can also refer to human resources and, as noted earlier, the teacher may need extra help with effective implementation of Internet tasks. Where school staff are not available, other school supports could be harnessed (see below).

Support and school culture

The best support helps teachers to help themselves or to get help from others. In this sense, support relates to the culture of the school, the availability of both formal and informal networking opportunities and the kind of openness and sharing that allows others who may wish to assist teachers and the school as a whole, such as parents and external organisations. The Internet's capacity for use as a communications tool is much underutilised in education, which still concentrates on its informational capacity. However, discussion groups, e-mail (regular and lists) and audio or video-conferencing on the Internet all offer huge potential for teachers and others to help themselves. Much of this potential is already apparent: the use of the Internet on a pan-European level for educator communication, information and project development is being very successfully demonstrated by the European Agency for Development in Special Needs Education through the conduct of the ICT research project among its member states. Resource centres, support groups, conferences and other dissemination events provide useful support, as do formal support structures such as the availability of advisers, help lines and technical backup.

The attitude of the school and its preparedness to address both ICT and inclusion are important factors to consider in relation to the Internet in special needs education. This manifests itself in the availability of the necessary infrastructure and resources, supportive management, principals and staff, and a school philosophy and practice which seek to work with others, to share ideas and to be flexible.

Research

The availability of research specific to Internet use by teachers is increasing, but statistical information specific to SEN and the Internet is also needed. This may prove to be a difficult task, given the individual nature of students' abilities and disabilities. Statistics on Internet use in special classes/units based in mainstream schools, or indeed on use by students with special needs in mainstream settings, are less available than special school statistics. However, it is in these settings where increasing numbers of students with special needs are being placed, in common with international trends, and the collection and analysis of data from the varied settings in which special needs students learn will also be needed to help determine future trends and needs.

Innovation and its uptake

Support of innovative teachers, schools and communities is another way both to promote the Internet in education and to study its use. The Organisation for Economic Co-operation and Development's Centre for Educational Research and Innovation (OECD/CERI) is conducting a study of school innovation and the quality of learning, focusing on ICT's impact on educational innovation and reform. The work in progress already indicates that innovation is usually led by one or two innovators and may take quite some time to spread to others. 'Without special intervention, diffusion throughout a school will take a number of years. Either a school must foster unusually high staff agreement, or an external agency with a specific mandate must play a major training role' (OECD/CERI 2001: 12). The latter is the case in Ireland, where the NCTE, in co-operation with local education centres and ICT advisers, has played a major training and support role in fostering innovation in the schools selected to participate in its Schools Integration Project. These schools have undertaken, as part of their project, the task of disseminating information to the wider school community. The OECD/CERI is looking at the spread of innovation within a school. But what indicators show best how to spread innovation from school to school? It is clear that simply disseminating results is not enough; concrete measures will need to be put in place to enable uptake of innovative ideas and practices by other schools. Policy makers must look at the extent to which they will need to provide funding and support, in relation to those made available to the initial innovators, in order to mainstream the innovation in other schools interested in taking up the innovative challenge.

Infrastructure

By far the most important variable in predicting teachers' Internet use is the teacher's level of classroom connectivity. . . . As schools move towards connecting more classrooms to the Internet, particularly with high-speed direct connections, we can foresee parallel increases in the number of teachers who make regular use of the Internet, particularly for student research, but also for their own class preparation and for student cross-classroom projects and Web publication.

(Becker 1999: 27)

Clearly, until there are more computers in the classroom connected to the Internet, teachers will not be able to use it to its full potential. Also, until the bandwidth issue is addressed, some teachers of students with special needs in particular will not find it practical to use because of the length of time one has to wait for a download and the discipline problems which can result. As well as more computers, special needs teachers need alternative input devices to enable their students to access the Web. The telecommunications cost issue is slowly being addressed in many countries. Flat-rate cost packages will generally be most suitable for schools with special needs students, as, depending on the nature of their disability, these students may take considerably longer to accomplish any Internet objectives than other students. Provision of teacher access to the Internet, whether through the school, the home, educational resource centres or through a loan system, is an essential component of this infrastructure. Those students who have the individual use of a computer as an assistive technology device may also need special access to the Internet.

Conclusion

The key point of this chapter was to address the question of how to advance the penetration of Internet use from the situation where a few advanced countries and a small number of schools and innovators in other countries use it extensively and others, especially those in special needs education, get left behind. Specific help and tailor-made solutions will be needed to assist the special education community. It may be tempting to simply avoid using the Internet until it becomes more user-friendly and until the necessary structures and supports are put in place. But to do so would be to put special needs students at a great disadvantage: 'teachers and learners excluded from it will become increasingly marginalised from an information economy whose wealth generation, intellectual as well as material, grows more dependent on it' (Yeomans 1996: 15). Those factors which shape access to conventional learning, such as awareness, user cost and competence, also shape access to learning via ICT, and learners excluded from ICT access will therefore be doubly disadvantaged (Yeomans 1996: 15). Certainly it is true that, as more schools and students 'get connected', those who are already somewhat excluded from the mainstream will become more so without access to ICT. Being on the Internet is fast becoming an essential element of an inclusive education, and everyone, from teachers to policy makers, has a part to play in making it happen.

Summary

* Progress towards inclusion varies internationally, as does the availability of the Internet in SEN settings.
* Some countries have made particular progress in these areas and others can learn from them.
* It is clear that the Internet has great potential as an enabler of inclusive practices and learning.
* Exclusion from the mainstream too often means exclusion from on-line life.
* All learners have an entitlement to Internet access.

References

Baysha, B. (1998) *The Internet: an Inclusive Magnet for Teaching all Students*, Oakland CA: World Institute on Disability, available on-line at www.wid.org/archives/handbook.pdf (accessed 27 July 2001).

Becker, H. J. (1999) 'Internet use by teachers: conditions of professional use and teacher-directed student use' in *Teaching, Learning and Computing: 1998 National Survey, Report No. 1*, Irvine MN: Center for Research on Information Technology and Organizations.

Berry, L. H. (2000) 'Cognitive effects of Web page design' in B. Abbey (ed.) *Instructional and Cognitive Impacts of Web-based Education*, Hershey PA: IDEA Group.

(Danish) Ministry of Education (1998) *Information and Communication Technologies in the Education System: Action Plan for 1998–2003*, Copenhagen: Ministry of Education.

Education Network Australia Schools Advisory Group (2000) *Learning in an On-line World: School Education Action Plan for the Information Economy*, Adelaide: Education Network Australia.

Franklin, B. (2000) 'Surf's up', *Interactive* 32, 42–44.

Goldstein, C. (1998) 'Learning at cyber camp' in *Teaching Exceptional Children*, May–June, 16–21.

Grey, D. (1999) *The Internet in School*, London: Cassell.

Grogan, Louise (2001), 'Opening up Windows of Opportunities for Students with Special Needs: an Overview of Information and Communication Technology, with Particular Reference to Students with a Moderate Learning Disability', unpublished Grad. Dip. ICT Ed. Thesis, University of Limerick.

Gunvall, P. (2000) *ICT in Education for Children with Disabilities in Sweden*, available on-line at www.european-agency.org/ict_sen_db/national_pages/attachments/ict.html (accessed on 1 July 2001).

IATSE (2000) *A National Survey of Special Needs Resource Teachers in Primary Schools*, Dublin: Irish Association of Teachers in Special Education.

(Irish) Department of Education and Science (1997) *Schools IT2000: a Policy Framework for the New Millennium*, Dublin: Government of Ireland.

Lamb, A., Smith, N., Johnson, L., and Smith W. L. (eds) (1998), *Surfin' the Internet: Practical Ideas from A to Z*, second edition, Emporia KS: Vision to Action.

MacMahon, A. (1998) *A Final Evaluation of the Horizon Project: Information Technology – Computer Training*, unpublished report to the Cystic Fibrosis Association of Ireland.

NCCA (1999) *Special Educational Needs: Curriculum Issues, Discussion Paper*, Dublin: National Council for Curriculum and Assessment.

NCTE (2000) *Innovative ICT Projects in Irish Schools: a Catalogue of Projects Supported by the Schools Integration Project under Schools IT2000*, Dublin: National Centre for Technology in Education.

OECD/CERI (2001) 'ICT: school innovation and the quality of learning – progress and pitfalls', brochure, available on-line at www.oecd.org/els/pdfs/EDSMINDOCA009.pdf (accessed on 28 July 2001).

Papert, S. (2001) 'Future of Learning: Let's be Serious', Speech at St Patrick's College of Education, Dublin, 19 June.

Smith, S., Boone, R., and Higgens, K. (1998) 'Expanding the writing process to the Web', *Teaching Exceptional Children*, May–June, 22–6.

(Swedish) Ministry of Education and Science (1998) *Tools for Learning: A National Programme for ICT in Schools*, Stockholm: Ministry of Education and Science.

Thornburg, D. (1996) *Putting the Web to Work: Transforming Education for the next Century*, n.p.: Starsong.

US Department of Education (2000) To assure the Free Appropriate Public Education of all Children with Disabilities: Twenty-second Annual Report to Congress on the Implementation of the Individuals with Disabilities Education Act, Washington DC: US Department of Education.

Yeomans, K. (1996) 'Learners on the Superhighway? Access to Learning via Electronic Communications', Winston Churchill Fellowship report, Leicester: National Institute of Adult Continuing Education.

Chapter 15

Moving forward

Chris Abbott

Perhaps the greatest change in thinking in special educational needs (SEN) circles in the 1990s was growing recognition that it is *inclusion*, not *integration*, which is our aim. Where once it seemed appropriate to argue for helping learners to change their behaviour or to accept inadequate support in order to be integrated, we now, quite rightly, expect that they will be included in the mainstream wherever possible. This will not be possible in many educational settings without considerable political will and increased resources. At a time when, in the UK at least, achievement seems to be measured through exam league tables, this resourcing seems to be less of a priority for government. Specialist and beacon schools too seem to have about them an aura of exclusion rather than inclusion, even if that may not be the intention.

The expression 'joined-up thinking' has become a political cliché but one that stands for an attitude of mind which is sorely needed. We have a plethora of educational initiatives and plans in the UK, most of them laudable in their own right, but too often incompatible with each other. If inclusion is to be our aim, as well as achievement and the celebration of excellence, it is vital to recognise all levels of achievement and celebrate all varieties of excellence. We have, in our special schools, a cohort of teachers and other professionals who can provide an excellent resource for the mainstream as we move, slowly but irrevocably, towards an inclusive future. The Internet can, as this book has attempted to show, help us to move along that path more quickly and to more effect. As Phelan has shown in the previous chapter, the Nordic countries in particular have been leaders in identifying the issues and then implementing change in this area. More recently Finland has begun to implement a national education Web portal which is symbolised and accessible to all (www.verkkosalkku.net), with any attempt to merely add alternative access seen as not good enough.

There can be very few people left within education who would still argue, as some once did (Stoll 1995), that the Internet is of only passing importance. Whatever form it may take in the future, the Internet or its successors have changed for ever our sense of how the peoples of the world are linked or separated. We have entered what Negroponte (1995) has called a 'post-geographical' phase, and it is one about which he is, on balance, optimistic.

> my optimism comes from the empowering nature of being digital. The access, the mobility, and the ability to effect change are what will make the future so different from the present. . . . As children appropriate a global information resource, and as they discover that only adults need learners' permits, we are bound to find new hope and dignity in places where very little existed before.
>
> (Negroponte 1995: 231)

'Hope and dignity' are exactly what our young people with special educational needs deserve, and must receive. The children we teach, members of what one writer (Tapscott 1998) has described as the Net generation, will expect the Internet to be a natural and expected part of their everyday learning experience. Learning with the support of digital media can be, and indeed should be, different from previous models of education. Tapscott describes what he terms the 'shifts of interactive learning', and although he is talking about all learners it is worth considering these shifts here.

1 From linear to hypermedia learning . . .
2 From instruction to construction and discovery . . .
3 From teacher-centred to learner-centred education . . .
4 From absorbing material to learning how to navigate and how to learn . . .
5 From school to lifelong learning . . .
6 From one-size-fits-all to customised learning . . .
7 From learning as torture to learning as fun . . .
8 From the teacher as transmitter to the teacher as facilitator . . .

(Tapscott 1998: 142–8)

Although some of these statements may seem rather too near the Internet hype which it has become fashionable to deny within education, there are also many echoes of developments within inclusive teaching. Teachers working with students with SEN have always worked in learner-centred ways. Learning how to learn has been a dominant focus, as has the expectation that learning continues after the compulsory school years. Many SEN teachers, often teaching way beyond their personal specialisms and subject expertise, have become facilitators long before their mainstream colleagues heard the term. If Tapscott's vision of the future of schooling is an accurate one, and much of what he says has become familiar from other policy documents and research papers, then teachers in SEN settings will be well placed to lead their colleagues into this interactive future.

With its support for interactive learning and inclusive practices, the Internet could do more than merely support inclusive practices within learning. Governments have agreed across international boundaries that inclusion is the way forward for the education of young people with special educational needs. The extent to which that inclusion has been achieved varies greatly from country to country, despite the fact that most countries of the world signed up to the Salamanca statement in 1994 (www.unesco.org/education/educprog/sne/salamanc/covere.html) and have therefore committed themselves to working towards inclusion. The long-term outcome of the use of on-line tools within education is likely to be a radical reinterpretation of the nature and location of schooling (Abbott 2000). Local primary schools, linked with their communities and playing a much wider role in those communities beyond present school hours, will certainly survive. There must be a question mark, however, against the future of the large secondary school: itself a product of the industrial age and now much criticised, and not as appropriate to the needs of a changed society. Specialist schools may indeed be a way forward and may come to be seen in hindsight as a temporary phase in the transformation of the secondary sector from a generalist schooling model to specialist subject-based learning centres which will be subsidiary to on-line distance education.

The special school – or inclusive education resource centre, as it will become – has an important and secure future. Using expertise already in existence, and following patterns already established in some such schools, these establishments will become true centres of excellence, facilitating learning by students and teachers, and leading curriculum reform with the aim of constantly enabling and supporting inclusion.

The Internet and inclusion will both have a large part to play in the education of young people with special educational needs in future. The extent to which the Internet may support the inclusion of these young learners has been the subject of this book, and it is clear from the contributions of such an experienced group of educators that there has been a mutually beneficial effect to date. Not only has the Internet supported the inclusion of learners, it has also put teachers in touch with colleagues outside the SEN area and has gone some way to deal with the feelings of isolation and separateness which existed when the Internet first became available within special education (Abbott and Cribb 2001).

Young people with physical disabilities need not only adapted and accessible buildings but also adaptive and accessible minds with which to communicate. The needs of people with sensory impairments need to be borne in mind not just by the designers of buildings but by the creators of learning resources, especially Web sites and other on-line facilities. Textbook writers and on-line resource creators must continually differentiate their offerings, as should curriculum designers and syllabus creators. Perhaps the biggest challenge for inclusion is the disaffection and emotional detachment characterised by the reaction of some young people to education: they are the learners least likely to be welcome in the mainstream unless appropriate resources and understanding have been developed.

The UK may have made mistakes in the area of ICT and the Internet, but most of them were the mistakes of those who go first; far better to have tried and only partially succeeded than never to have tried at all. National initiatives like the Inclusion site, LEA intranets and international links, all discussed in this volume, offer considerable potential for building on this expertise and linking it with inclusive practice. As we move into a new phase of inclusion, with a new SEN Code of Practice in the UK and continuing developments in inclusive practice across the world, it will remain important to use new technologies such as the Internet in order to share good practice and inform each other – for the benefit of all learners.

References

Abbott, C. (2000) *ICT: Changing Education*, London: RoutledgeFalmer.
Abbott, C. (2001) 'Special educational needs: becoming more inclusive' in J. Dillon and M. Maguire (eds) *Becoming a Teacher: Issues in Secondary Teaching*, second edition, Buckingham: Open University Press.
Abbott, C., and Cribb, A. (2001) 'Special schools, inclusion and the World Wide Web: the emerging research agenda', *British Journal of Educational Technology* 32 (3), 331–42.
Negroponte, N. (1995) *Being Digital*, London: Coronet.

Stoll, C. (1995) *Silicon Snake Oil: Second Thoughts on the Information Superhighway*, London: Macmillan.

Tapscott, D. (1998) *Growing up Digital: The Rise of the Net Generation*, New York: McGraw-Hill.

Glossary

Adobe Acrobat reader A software program which is free to download and enables a user to read protected documents but not change them.

applet A small program which is needed before some components of complex Web pages will operate.

bitmap An image format; files end in .BMP.

broadband Common term used to describe any Internet connection by wireless, cable or other technology which is appreciably faster than a standard telephone line.

browser A software program which allows a user to access the World Wide Web. The two best-known browsers are Netscape Communicator and Internet Explorer.

digital camera A camera which saves images as a file rather than onto photographic file; these images can be copied and manipulated using a graphics program.

GIF An image format which is best used for line diagrams rather than photographs. Files will end in .GIF.

homepage The beginning or entry area of a World Wide Web site.

HTML Hyper Text Mark-up Language: the code in which Web pages are written. Although it is possible to write pages in code, most home users do not do so, preferring to use a Web authoring program.

ICT Information and Communication Technology.

Internet A general term covering a range of on-line tools and environments, including e-mail, file transfer, real-time chat and the World Wide Web.

intranet A computer network which may look like the Web but is available only within a company or institution and whose employees or members may need to access by use of a password.

IT Information Technology.

JAVA   Computer language used to add extra functionality to Web sites. Java may slow page-loading, but if it is switched off the page may not be usable.

JPG/JPEG   An image format often used for photographs on Web sites. Files will end in .JPG.

MIDI   A format in which digitised music and sounds are stored.

NGfL   The National Grid for Learning. As local grids are developed around the UK, the NGfL's role is changing so that it becomes a grid of grids rather than a resource repository in its own right.

NOF   New Opportunities Fund, set up by the UK government to use National Lottery income for the public good.

overlay   Paper sheet with images or text which is placed on an overlay keyboard.

overlay keyboard   Known as a membrane keyboard in some countries; a keyboard alternative consisting of a flat pad with a large number of pressure-sensitive areas. Sometimes called a Concept Keyboard (after a major manufacturer).

plug-in   Extra program which can be downloaded to work in tandem with a Web browser to display extra audio, video or other functions.

PDF   The extension at the end of an Acrobat file which must be read with the Adobe Acrobat reader.

screen reader   Software which converts words on the screen into spoken text.

surfing   Moving from site to site on the Web by clicking on links; a term used disparagingly by some and positively by others, much as real-life ocean surfing could be seen as the height of indolence or the meaning of life . . .

Switch   Keyboard alternative which comes in many forms (large, small, mat, light, movement etc) and can be operated by users who are unable to select and press keys.

URL   Uniform Resource Locator – the address of a Web site.

Web/World Wide Web/WWW   Often used synonymously with the Internet, but actually just that part of it which is accessible through the use of a Web browser. It was the Web which made the Internet accessible and led to its rapid adoption outside academic and government circles in the 1990s.

Web site   The pages which make up a bank of resources about a company, institution or individual.

Word Viewer   A free-to-download program which enables users who do not own Microsoft Word to view, but not change, Word files they have downloaded.

Writing with Symbols 2000   A symbol processor which enables text and symbols to be linked, resources to be created and enables symbol users to communicate with others.

Index